Gone Fishin'...

For Beginners

How To Look Forward To Retirement

How To Keep The Kids Off The Street

OR... How Everyone Can Enjoy Themselves

Gone Fishin'... For Beginners

How To Look Forward To Retirement

How To Keep The Kids Off The Street

OR... How Everyone Can Enjoy Themselves

By Manny Luftglass

Gone Fishin' Enterprises
PO Box 556, Annandale, New Jersey 08801

Pictured on the cover: *(On the left.)* Dayne Hippensteel from Poinciana, Florida. *(In the middle.)* Marilyn Suss with a 6-pound fluke on her first fluke trip ever aboard the *Hey Jude* with Captain Judie Schoerlin out of Shinnecock Bay, New York. *(On the right.)* New London, Connecticut PBA Vice President Clayton Sizer helping a girl take a snapper blue off her hook at a fishing derby.

Pictured on the back cover: Ray Willington holding a fine mature 9-pounder in the HOH River.

Gone Fishin' ... For Beginners

By Manny Luftglass

© 2003 Emanuel Luftglass

Published By
Gone Fishin' Enterprises
PO Box 556, Annandale, New Jersey 08801

ISBN: 0-9650261-9-1

UPC: 793380 19356-0

Photo Credits:
Captain Morgan's B&T, Madison, CT; Captain Judie Schoerlin *Hey Jude*, Shinnecock, NY;
New London CT Police Department; Denny's Guide Service, Sitka, AK; Guide Mike Schmitz, Jr.,
Forks, WA; Ray's Guide Service, Dupont, PA; Penn Fishing Tackle, Philadelphia, PA; Bernie's Fishing
Tackle, Brooklyn, NY; Fish307.com Lake George, NY; O. Mustad & Son, Auburn, NY; Fish 'N Tales,
Wrightstown, PA; Ron Jacobsen, NJ Division of Fish & Wildlife, Hackettstown, NJ; Ande Line, courtesy
of Efinger Sporting Goods, Bound Brook, NJ; Murphy's Guide Service, Lake Conroe, TX; Deborah
Flanagan, Martinsville, NJ; Jen Zook, Readington Township, NJ; David Sandler, Flagtown, NJ;
and from my own collection.

Author Credit: Joe Perrone (fly fishing section).

Design & Typography:
TeleSet
Hillsborough, New Jersey

PRINTED IN THE UNITED STATES OF AMERICA

As a lifelong fisherman
(and that involves lots of years of life, dear readers),
I would like to dedicate this book
to all of you who have not yet enjoyed my favorite hobby.

If you haven't tried it yet,
I sincerely hope that you will feel the love
I have for my favorite sport through my words,
and realize that something really wonderful
lies ahead.

Contents

CHAPTER 1: **Which Beginners?** **10**
    Retired Or About To Be Retired 10
    Juniors 05
        SQUEAMISH KIDS 21
        MACHO KIDS 21
    Everyone Else 22

CHAPTER 2: **Bait** **24**
    Bait For Anyone 24
        CORN 24
        DOUGHBALLS 24
        CORNMEAL BAIT 25
        STORE-BOUGHT BAITS 26
        SALMON EGGS 26
        POWER BAIT 26
        MARSHMALLOWS 26
        BREAD 27
        LIVER 27
    Dead Bait 27
    Live Bait For The Strong Of Heart 28
        FISH 28
        WIDE AND WHITE 28
        SHRIMP/CRAWFISH 29
        EELS 31
        WORMS 31

CHAPTER 3: **Chumming In Freshwater** **32**

CHAPTER 4: **Tackle** **34**
    The "Can Man" Way 34
    Pole Fishin' 35
    Reel Fishing 35
        REVOLVING SPOOL REELS 35
        LEVEL-WIND REELS 36
        FAST/SLOW RETRIEVE REELS 37
        FIXED SPOOL REELS 37
        FLY REELS 39
    "Drag" 39
    Oil 41
    Fishing Poles — The Reel's Partner 41
        FLY RODS 41
    What Is Fly Fishing And What Do I Need
        To Get Started? *By Joe Perrone* 42
        FLY LINES 42

FLY RODS 43
REELS 43
TERMINAL TACKLE 44
NYMPHS, STREAMERS AND FLIES? 44
IN CONCLUSION 44
BAIT CASTING RODS 45
SPINNING OR SPIN-CAST RODS 46
CONVENTIONAL RODS 47
PACK RODS 47
The Good With The Bad 48

CHAPTER 5: **Balance** **50**
Rod To Reel 50
Line To Reel 51
Casting 53

CHAPTER 6: **Types Of Line** **54**

CHAPTER 7: **Freshwater Fishing** **56**
Lakes And Ponds 56
DOUBLE-ANCHORING 57
SINGLE-ANCHORING 60
SINGLE, ON A "BRIDLE:" .60
DRIFTING 61
TROLLING 61
Rivers And Streams 63
DOUBLE-ANCHORING 63
BRIDLE-ANCHORING 63
ANCHORING ON A SLOPE 65
ANCHORING ON OBSTRUCTIONS 65
Pay Ponds And Waters 66
Fishing Derbies 66

CHAPTER 8: **How To Hook 'Em** **68**

CHAPTER 9: **Hook Removal** **71**

CHAPTER 10: **Clothing** **72**
Clothing For Cold Times .72
Clothing For Much Saner Times 76
Saltwater Clothing 77

CHAPTER 11: **Freshwater Boats** **78**
Small Water 78
Big Water 79
Engines 81
SHORE FISHING 82

CHAPTER 12: **Saltwater Fishing** **84**
"Charter" Boats 84
"Open And Head" Boats .85

DRIFTING 87
THE ANGLE 88
ANCHORED 88
CHUMMING 89
ROTATE FISH 89
Fishing From Land And Piers 89
CHAPTER 13: Terminal Tackle (Fresh & Saltwater) **91**
LURES 91
"Stickbaits" 91
Soft Lures 92
Metal Lures 92
Flies 93
Floats 93
BOBBERS 93
"Slider" Floats 95
Sinkers 95
BANK SINKERS 95
PYRAMID SINKERS 95
ROUND SINKERS 96
BELL SINKERS 96
EGG SINKERS 96
PINCH-ON SINKERS 97
Swivels 97
SNAP-SWIVELS 97
THREE-WAY SWIVELS 97
BARREL-SWIVELS 98
FISH-FINDER RIGS 98
Leaders 98
Hooks 99
Knots 100
Here's How To Tie An Improved Clinch Knot 101
Here's How To Tie A Simplified Barrel Or Blood Knot .102
CHAPTER 14: Fish Cleaning **103**
CHAPTER 15: Cooking Fish **108**
Fried Fish 108
Sautéed Fish 111
In The Oven 111
"Whole" And On The Bone 111
CHAPTER 16: The License **112**
CHAPTER 17: "Catch And Release" **114**
CHAPTER 18: Mounting **117**
CHAPTER 19: Find A Friend **119**
CHAPTER 20: Still More **121**
Lateral Line Vs. "Vibration Time" 121
Solunar Time 123
Checklist 124

Foreword

The intent is to "hook" people with this book who either have never gone fishing, or better yet, folks who have tried it with so little success that they swore that they would never go fishing again. By buying this book, you have dared me to interest you in the most popular sport in America and I hope to meet the challenge and make you into fishermen. No, not necessarily anglers who are consistently awake an hour before the alarm goes off that day. And no, not an outdoorsman who tosses and turns all night in anticipation. In fact, I seek to share my knowledge and skill with you so that you can find another thing to do for fun — not making fishing #1 if you don't want it to be that — just something else to enjoy!!

According to the 2001 national survey conducted by the U.S. Fish and Wildlife Service, 34,071,000 people went fishing somewhere in America that year! They spent part of 557,394,000 days on the water. And even more impressive, the American Sportfishing Association quoted a recent Harris Poll that said fishing was ranked the most popular outdoor activity in America. The A.S.A. study showed a total of 44 million Americans who fish spend nearly $42 billion per year on fishing equipment.

Chances are that in Great Britain, Canada and elsewhere,

similar numbers of anglers pounded the water with everything from flies to corn to who-knows-what else. To note: British subjects who use rod and reel call themselves "Anglers" — those who fish commercially are "Fishermen."

More people go fishing in America than the people who participate in the next two most popular sports put together! Just for example, only 13 million people hunted in the United States in 2001. So if you haven't gotten out yet for the first time, or better, if you didn't like it when you went, please read this book and learn how to get a share of the pleasure that thirty-four million people got! (Or maybe forty-four million, if you go with the A.S.A. study.)

By the way, you will notice that at times, I separate fresh from saltwater fishing, and at other times, we talk about them together. There are many things about fishing that really don't differ, salt or fresh, and that is why I lump both together sometimes. I hope this helps rather than confuses you!

CHAPTER 1

Which Beginners?

Retired Or About To Be Retired

There are many millions of retired citizens all over the world who have recently stopped working. So many of these people were truly unprepared for the event. Yes, a good percentage were financially in shape but chances are good to excellent that the ones that were okay, money-wise, had not prepared themselves with something to do after they retired. Worse off yet are those who were rather forcibly retired — by any other name, laid off, etc., out of work!

So you had a list of states and countries that you wanted to visit. And yes, a sheet with names and address of relatives and friends who you wanted to spend time with. You have gone through both lists, or maybe worse, are near the end of the lists and dread the future.

This book is for you! Volunteer work at your place of worship can be very rewarding. Pushing a cart for free at your neighborhood hospital, giving out magazines, etc., is very nice. A friend of mine sits in a little cubicle at an airport and gives directions to travelers who recently arrived for land transportation and the like and this volunteerism is both rewarding and appreciated.

This New Yorker didn't know how to rig up so I showed him how and he beat me out for the pool on his first trip on the Blue Heron 101 out of Riviera Beach, Florida.

But — volunteerism goes only so far ... a void remains!

Millions of people who are approaching retirement age are terrified because they simply don't have anything else to do once they take off the ties or high-heeled shoes.

Retired or about to retire? Look forward to it with a smile on your face, because fishing can be just what the doctor ordered for you. If you are in sufficiently satisfactory health, a myriad of opportunities lies ahead.

Retired at 55? Wow, am I ever jealous of you. I didn't do it until a bit later. Are you hanging 'em up at 60? You have so many excellent years ahead. 65? The typical age for most people to step down is at 65, and with a program in your future that involves fishing, you might find that years of pleasure are on the horizon!

The average woman lives to age 80 or so, and men can expect

to go to 72, but those numbers aren't always applicable. These averages apply to people who start off at a far younger age. If you take people who are 50 and project their expected remaining number of years, you will find that women will go well past age 80. Men will clearly exceed 72 by quite a few years (and here we are going with the average senior citizen, not with those who have a bright star shining in their future). People who have fishing in their lives are expected to exceed all of the usual projections, count on it!

At last look, 21% of anglers are age 55 or older. If you are not among that large number, it's time to do it now! In America, fishermen spent $40,000,000,000. Yes, you can probably buy all the fish you will be able to eat for less than you might spend catching them. But the fish you catch fresh will taste better, and you can also grab lots of healthy fresh air and exercise along the way.

Senior citizens have fishing clubs of their own, or can join clubs that accept folks of any age. However, from personal experience I have found that more than one-half of the members of clubs that I visit are age 55 or far older. The camaraderie that is gained through such clubs is immeasurable.

Let's face it, as a "senior," one might also be a little concerned about fishing alone. Driving to and from a venue without company can also be daunting. This is where a club can be invaluable. You can participate in club events — charters, exotic trips, etc, or merely befriend someone else and share the driving.

Elder people have access to Adult Education classes that are taught through thousands of high schools and colleges clear across the land. You don't have to hire a guide to teach you — a three-night, ten-student class on fishing could fill in lots of the gaps.

Buying subscriptions to the dozens of magazines out there can also help, but you may find that most of the articles are written for fishermen with considerable experience. But a visit to your library may be even better. Ask the "Reference Librarian" to help you find magazine articles in fishing publications found in their libraries that target "beginners," or better, "senior beginners." Any library of size will have quite a bit of material to check out. Be certain that

Brian Lull and his father Richard. Richard was quite ill when
he and his son fished out of Sitka, Alaska, his birthplace, with
Denny's Guide Service. Richard caught his first big halibut
(among other fish) that day. Unfortunately, Richard has passed on.

you make the visit to the library on a weekday rather than a busy evening or worse, on a Saturday. The Reference Librarian is an invaluable source of assistance, but only when she/he isn't too busy!

Fishing can fill in the void left by retirement, and you can spend as many or as few days doing it as you wish. Remember the survey quoted from earlier? The average number of days that anglers actually got out on the water in 2001 was 16. So if you "only" hit the average, you just got something fun to do for 16 days a year. Of course if the fishing bug bites you, that number can be dramatically increased. For example, I went fishing in excess of 125 days in 2002!

A wise man once said that days out fishing don't count towards life expectancy. Simply put, I expect to dramatically increase my number of days' fishing count for years to come, if only to achieve longer and happier life!

Juniors

If you are a youngster who likes to read a book, check out what is to follow. On the other hand, if you are a parent or guardian and are anxious to get your young person into something that can be a most enjoyable and pleasant pastime, you may want to also pay close attention, please!

My first recollection of a fishing outing goes back to the winter of 1938 on a cold night in Brooklyn. My parents, brother and I drove to Coney Island, bought some bait, and walked out onto Steeplechase Pier. And as many years back as that was, and as young as I was (3+ years of age), I really remember most of the evening! We shared two rods and reels and passed them back and forth with each fish caught. The tally for the evening was a fine mess of whiting ("silver hake") and they made for a great meal.

I am not here to suggest that you start a kid off at night in the winter, because that could end the whole deal before it begins. But it worked for me because the evening was not very cold and the fish were biting, and because our whole family was out together. As young as I was, I really think that the family thing made it work best.

Kids today have so many things to do without parents, but taking your child fishing is a wonderful bonding experience, if you do it right. Frankly, you could write a book on the subject (and I did just that with my friend Joe Perrone). To get the whole story rather than just the few pages that follow, try to scare up a copy of that book. If you cannot find it at a chain store or through Amazon, etc., the order form in the back of this book will tell you how to get it (autographed too!) The name of the book is "Gone Fishin'...With Kids" and Joe came up with its great sub-title — "How To Take Your Kid Fishing And Still Be Friends." It retails at only $9.99.

Okay, advertisement over, back to taking a child fishing, or if the young person is old enough, how to go about doing it all by himself.

Start your young person out with a virtual guarantee of a catch! A "written guarantee" is, of course, impossible, but you can come close. Presuming that your child is five years old or more (and smaller ones can do it too, probably), find yourself a "pay pond." Every state in the country (and lots of other countries all over the world) has private lakes or ponds that are well stocked with fish. Some hold species that reproduce naturally and others are purchased and dropped into the water by the pond's management. But the bottom line of all this is that the water holds fish, hungry fish, and a kid may like being outdoors with mom or dad, but once a fish takes that bobber down, wild excitement usually follows and improves the day further.

Look in your yellow pages to start. The wider the area your book covers, the better the chance at finding what you want to locate. Look under "Fishing," "Bait & Tackle," etc., and you will probably find someone who can help, if not the number of such a pond itself. If all else fails, call your state's Department of Fish and Game, go through the maze called "Government," and someone will probably be able to give you the name and phone number of a few spots that are not far from your home. I have found such facilities in many states and I know that a variety of "pay waters" exists throughout Great Britain. If you are good on the computer, just look "pay ponds" up on the Internet. I bet you will find three or four that are within an hour or two from your home.

Why did I spend so much time on this subject? Well, so that you can put your little one into some fish! If you don't have your own rod and reel, most of these facilities will rent an outfit to you as part of the cost of admission. You can buy hooks, floats, bait — the whole deal there.

And now comes the second most important lesson regarding "pay ponds." #1 is that you can catch fish. #2 is that you gotta' pay for them! Most pay ponds require you to keep many if not all of the fish that you catch and they charge you, as a rule of thumb, X many dollars per pound.

Here you are at the "Gotbucks" Pay Lake, and are they biting, or what? Little Janie is deep into catching trout and she really loves it. And what was that you said? "Enough?" Say what? It is critically important that you have a heart to heart talk with your child before you reach the lake of choice about money! You have to be ready to take them away ten minutes after starting, if that is what they want, but they too must know that you may ask them to stop fishing, on the other hand. They may have to be required to quit, unless you want to hock your socks! Again, talk about it at home and then in the car. Set a dollar limit or maybe a take home fish count limit. A single trout could cost two or three bucks but what if the catch reaches a dozen? What can you do with so many fish and do you have enough cash with you to pay for them?

SHH: Summing it all up, if you ever want to improve your odds at getting a youngster interested in fishing, get them to a pay pond! By the way, the emphasis here is on the word "pond or lake," not stream. A body of moving water may hold thousands of fish but if the child never went fishing before, even if you are a pro, they simply won't be able to handle the subject of current or moving water.

Last but not least about "pay ponds" is the fact that 99% of them are not ringed with hook-grabbing tree branches. It is not only annoying and embarrassing to get your float, etc., hung up; it can also be quite dangerous.

Besides pay ponds as a fine starting out venue, a private charter may be a good second choice. Now don't go about chartering a boat that travels a bazillion miles offshore and stays out there until everyone has passed out from catching so many fish (or has nothing left in their stomachs from throwing up, more likely.) You should set up a charter in the time of the year that the weather is best and the fish are biting.

All of the fishing magazines that I know of have advertisements that say how many hours the boats spend on the water, and what their sailing times are. Some go for four hours, others for six, and so on. If you are near an ocean, or a big lake, a four-hour charter may be just what you want to get little Johnny started, providing you and the skipper have a clear understanding of who is the boss. If you chartered the boat and ten minutes out, the kid starts saying those dreaded words — "Is it time to go home yet?" you have to bite your tongue and ask the captain to head for the barn. Yes, you will lose your money, and the captain may get cranky because his best advertisement is to display a fine catch when the boat ties up, but if you ever want a chance at getting the kid out again, you really must listen and obey. Even worse would be if the child (OR YOU) gets seasick. If the little one wants to go home, make sure the skipper is so directed, and next time, hopefully, with calmer winds, the water may be flat like a millpond.

Charters are usually booked weeks in advance, so you can't really pick a "good wind and weather" day that way. If "headboats" are not far away, (boats that take individual walk-on customers that very day), this may be the answer. If you wake up and the weather report is for mild temperatures and light wind, go for it! However, no matter what, if fishing is good or bad, or Johnny (OR YOU) get seasick, the boat stays out until the Captain says it is time to go back to the dock. Therefore, please do pick the day with extreme care.

If you are making your second or third fishing trip with the little one on board a boat, just use your head. Make it an afternoon trip, not one that begins at dawn. Make certain the boat fishes in protected water, not way out in the middle of nowhere where the wind can blow so hard that it can create gigantic urpher-sized waves.

And under any and all circumstances, carry some manner of

seasick protection with you. Talk to your family doctor to get advice on what works best. Some people wear ear patches, others go with something leather around their wrists, and still more take old-fashioned seasick pills. Be certain that your little one takes a kid-sized dose of whatever you buy, though.

The very best insurance against seasickness is a gang of hungry fish. But a key to success, besides medication and action, is to stay on deck. If the boat is big, meaning it has a cabin or even a comfortable below deck section, keep out!

SHH: Adequately protected from wind and spray, your young person should be in the stern of the boat, and concentrating on the sky, not the wave action to the water. While many kids want to head up forward like the young lady in Titanic, the waves are born there, and any kind of rock and roll will be greatly exaggerated in the front of the boat. The flattest seas are felt right up against the railing in the back of the boat!

Still more anti-barf insurance is obtained through several sources, sleep and food. A good, solid eight hours of sleep is the best thing you can get to help avoid getting sick. Sure, lots of people toss and turn before undertaking something exciting, but do try to give your ward a chance at a minimum of eight hours sleep.

This one really applies to everyone, not to children alone — from a food standpoint, grease equals trouble, most of the time. So be sure the breakfast is not heavy, but adequate. And be certain to have a few snacks, sandwiches, and soda with you to fill in the quiet times. I used to bring a whole variety of goodies when I started my daughter Barbara off and it really did help.

SHH: My own sandwiches are wrapped in separate halves. And you ask why? Hey, listen, you may get to be as wacky about fishing as I am. In the past, all too often, I would be eating lunch and a fish would bite. (Do I stop fishing and take the rod out while eating? Of course not!) In my excitement I found myself dropping the sandwich and usually it wound up on the wet deck of the boat, or in the dirt at shore. So now I have the sandwiches cut and if I drop part of one half, at least I have the other half to eat.

Oh yes, one more thing that will help keep the little one from

Squeamish kids? Not my grandchildren! (Well, maybe.)
(Top) Hunter Kane. (Bottom) Hartley Zook and Elizabeth Kane.
(Top next page) Madison Zook.

wanting to go home — any manner of portable toilet that you can find. The charter and headboats all come well equipped, of course, but for kids (or yourself), have something with you that can serve as a container, as well as a goodly supply of toilet tissue.

SQUEAMISH KIDS: Don't force a kid to bait a hook, or to take a fish off the hook. And maybe not even to handle a fish or a piece of bait. Some take to all of this like a duck to water, but others may really get upset at the mere thought. However, on the second or third outing, try again, gently, and you may find that the little one is ready and willing, and curious enough to try it out.

MACHO KIDS: Self-explanatory, really, is this subject. But make sure that the proper method of baiting or hook removing is very carefully explained first. Getting stuck by the gill plate or dorsal fin of even a little sunfish can hurt like all get out, so teach (or maybe learn first) how to hold a fish. Little hands may require two of them to hold the fish, while you may need just one. But the key is to make a sandwich around the fish so that it can be firmly held but yet securely enough so that no one gets finned. Some fish can stick you worse than others, like catfish and a variety of tropical water species. When in doubt, buy one of those fish holders that are available in tackle stores that form a protective ring around the fish. Then she can remove the hook without making her bleed.

We will talk later about how to deal with hook removal.

Everyone Else

We have talked about the oldsters and youngsters at length. That leaves everyone else, and for certain these potential anglers form the largest group. So if you are between, for example, 18 and 55, and in good health, make sure you have finished reading everything up to now, but concentrate even more because this section is for you!

What is fishing? It is relaxation or exercise, whatever you want it to be. You can go fishing to escape from the job or trouble at home, or maybe to try to forget about money or health problems. It can clear out your brain from any and all other thoughts, if you let it bite that deeply into you. However, you can also use fishing as a hobby that challenges your mind and body, as well as a sport that can put food on the table. The list of reasons for going out fishing is endless, and if you get into it like me, you may be able to add a few items to the list as well. The key is to fish as much as you both want to and can do. Once a month? No problem, do it. Only on "Opening Day" to enjoy the camaraderie? Hey, go for it. But if you find yourself being hooked and you want to fish at least once a week, or even every other day, you may be approaching Manny Madness level! The only cure for this is to succumb to it.

Yes, a two to four week trip out of San Diego down Mexico way can seem like a lifetime, especially if seasickness hits. Sure, a two-day adventure up to George's Bank offshore of New England might be a bit too much. And if you are on a big boat that heads down to the Dry Tortugas from a South Florida port and the waves start crashing over the bow only a few hours out, you may have wanted to concentrate more on golf or tennis. But again, make adjustments in your schedule to fit your physical abilities and financial condition, as well as how such outings might affect your family life, and — go do it! You just might discover that you love fishing! The fresh, clean air alone could be worth its weight in gold.

Much of what you read herein will overlap from salt to fresh-water fishing, of course. But there certainly are things that more apply to one than the other, therefore, let's separate the two for a while now, okay?

CHAPTER 2

Bait

Since the focus here is towards beginners, we won't get into some of the more exotic types of bait. But for most species of fish in most waters, there really are several specific varieties of each to talk about. First, let's discuss bait fishing in general — concentrating on freshwater stuff.

Bait For Anyone

CORN: "Bait" can be alive or dead, and for that matter, could have never even been alive. For example, in many freshwater venues, one of the best kinds of bait is the plain old "can 'o corn!" Fishermen all over the world have been known to catch anything from trout to carp on a few kernels of corn. So if you are among the beginners who aren't anxious to hold onto something that is wiggling and then try to impale it with a hook, take note — corn is for you!

DOUGHBALLS: I've caught trout, chub and good-sized carp on doughballs and again, if you don't want to stick a hook into a worm, try a doughball. The standard mixture would consist of a little mixing bowl with three items alongside. First is flour, next comes sugar, and last is your "smell." For simplicity sake, go with vanilla extract. However, your doughball can be flavored with any kind of odor you want to add in.

Put several heaping spoonfuls of flour into the bowl and then add some water. It's trial and error but after a while, you will get the hang of it quickly. Add in a little sugar and use the flat side of your spoon to mix water and flour together into a paste. Make sure you eliminate all lumps and now add a dash of vanilla. This will increase the moisture content too high so add another tablespoonful of flour. The idea is to get a final mixture that is smooth and pleasantly odorous but yet easy to pull a piece off and put on a hook. Start with a large ball of bait and simply pinch off enough to mold onto your hook.

If the bait doesn't stick well to the hook, the mixture is either too wet or dry so adjust accordingly.

CORNMEAL BAIT: Catfish will often compete aggressively for this bait but its primary intent is to be used as carp bait. Since carp are caught all across the world, this bait can produce fun for you worldwide. The mixture here involves the elements noted above — flour, sugar, vanilla (or other nice smells like chocolate or anise), and water. Add to the ready ingredients a box of yellow cornmeal. (You can also use white cornmeal another day). Instead of making this a "raw" mixture, let's cook up some bait.

Find a nasty old pot somewhere in the back reaches of the cupboard and drag it out. Alternatively, buy one — the porcelain variety might be best. Put 2-3 inches of water in the pot and bring it to a boil. Drop in several heaping tablespoonfuls of cornmeal and immediately add one filled with flour. Turn the heat down halfway and now mix like the dickens to get all the powder wet down. This will really take more trial and error than making doughballs, but view it as fun and you will get the idea soon enough. Put a teaspoon filled with sugar into the pot and then drop in some vanilla. And again, mix — quickly.

Take everything out of the pot in pieces and knead each hunk separately before making a single large mass out of it all. Your finished bait will be smooth with no lumps and can be formed up into a round ball. Test it by pinching off a piece and roll it into a very small ball. This ball could then be used as bait by pushing your hook into it and molding it around the hook into a pear-shaped hunk of bait. If you don't think the ball is okay, either start over again or simply add more mix — wet or dry. The bait ball should be quickly wrapped in aluminum foil to prevent it from drying out.

STORE-BOUGHT BAITS: Among other companies, "Uncle Josh" and "Berkley" package pre-flavored baits and they come in a variety of odors depending on what kind of fish you seek. "Carp baits" usually have vanilla or cheese in them, and a preservative is added as well which allows you to simply place the cover back on the container for use again another day. These and other companies also package "stink" baits for catfish and the like.

SALMON EGGS: While purists swear that they catch the biggest and most trout, salmon, etc., on eggs or egg skeins that they gathered themselves from fresh caught fish, let's just go with another store-bought bait, the typical salmon egg jar. Many a company is out there that vacuum packs eggs into air-tight jars that can be kept from season to season if not in too cold or hot a space. The eggs come in natural colors or are died any manner of color that comes to the mind of the company. The more typical colors are pink, natural or orange. An addition to the mix that really has brought improved catch totals is some shrimp flavoring. Pink shrimp eggs were the best bait around for the early 2000's!

"POWER BAIT:" The folks at Berkley created baits that are easy to handle and inoffensive to use. Somewhere in the back of their basement lab (well, probably not a basement at all, but it sounds better), a mad scientist came up with a variety of mixtures and colors and this stuff works! You can buy pellets or hunks, colored or "natural," and the thing that makes it all good, besides smell, is that the stuff floats! So fish will eat these offerings because they are attractive and smell nice, but some of us feel that the main reason is because they are easy to see because they float!

MARSHMALLOWS: Yes, marshmallows do make good bait in freshwater with the focus on trout, but some fishermen use them for salmon and others catch carp and catfish on them. There are marshmallows that are packaged specifically as bait and many of these are flavored. Some come smelling like vanilla and others have the odor of cheese. But as with "Power Bait," one of the main attractions to a marshmallow is its visibility, because it floats!

The best 'mallows to use, by far, are the miniature variety. Unless you are after really big freshwater fish, concentrate your attention on the smaller ones as bait. Most of these come in white color only, but from time to time, you may find your favorite supermarket carries them in assorted colors. Chances are good that around Halloween in particular is a time to find the variety of colors.

SHH: Here's my basic rule of thumb regarding color — if you are after carp, concentrate on the use of the yellow ones, because they look like corn. For trout or salmon, go with either the orange or pink ones. And that will leave you with a lot of green colored marshmallows. Save these for the kid that you bring with you. In this way, you can keep her hands away from your bait and still provide some snacks to keep a smile on her face. All kidding aside, think pink or orange for salmonoids and yellow for carp. Save the greenies for Jennie and Johnnie.

BREAD: Once more we talk about floating bait. Yes, bread doesn't have to float, but some of the best uses of it relate specifically to the bait bobbing up and down on top while a wary fish observes it from below. Carp are the main fish that go after floating bread and to be even more specific, a piece of a bagel often is best yet. Bread that floats on still or moving water is natural to the extent that most fish have observed it. Sure, bread is not natural because it can't swim but other than in the most rustic of locations, every fish has seen bread floating by overhead. The sight of a carp sucking in a piece of floating bagel or bread can get a "carpers" knees knocking!

LIVER: Yeah, liver. Sure, the little kids may not like it but fish certainly do. Freshwater fish of every type will hit a chunk of liver. Nasty old stinky liver will produce catfish when nothing else will work at all. And fresh liver will be attacked with vigor often by hybrid bass, true-strain striped bass, sunfish, and even smallmouth bass. My guess is that I've personally caught better than 100 trout on liver as well.

Dead Bait

Everything else noted above is used in freshwater fishing usually, but since lots of you will want to fish in saltwater, let's discuss dead baits, the kinds that were once alive but you didn't have to kill them yourselves. Dead baits can be found in a variety of shapes and sizes and are used in salt or sweetwater.

Typical dead baits are small fish, or shrimp, generally frozen, and while you may get some stink on your fingers, at least you will not have impaled a living creature. (By the way, remember my excuse noted below — no eyelids equal no "real" pain anyway okay?)

Pieces of a shedder crab make spectacular bait in saltwater rivers and bays for a wide variety of fish. And as for dead shrimp, this stuff is productive for yet more fish in saltwater, as well as fresh. I've caught channel catfish on shrimp in sweetwater, and all types of critters in the brine.

SHH: Here's a secret regarding dead shrimp — peel 'em! Whether you are using the entire peeled shrimp or just a piece, fish will respond much better if you remove the shell because the smell is much stronger.

Live Bait For The Strong Of Heart

First, start off with the basic concept that if the critter you are about to impale doesn't have any eyelids it really cannot feel pain like humans do, okay? And now work your way out from there. If, however, handling live bait won't work for you, there are other options — lure fishing, dead or never alive bait, or maybe asking your companion or mate to bait the hook while you turn your head around and look the other way.

FISH: As for bait fishing, for the most part, the bigger fish are caught on live bait. However, carpet-sized halibut are caught often by using the head and entrails of salmon as bait. Sure, some fish will eat anything at all. The monster-sized catfish caught in the southern part of the United States are often caught on some old stinky mass of meat and guts, but again, most bigger fish like big, live baitfish.

WIDE AND WHITE: And here is something to take careful note of regarding how to keep your baitfish alive in warm times when they might otherwise croak. The main components are white containers and ice, plus new water.

You know those old circular metal buckets that float? They have a removable insert and in cool times, lots of baitfish can be kept alive that way. The floating plastic yellow buckets work the same way, but if it is warm out, bordering on too warm, most of your baitfish will die. The surface water could be just too hot for the bait to live. So at such times, it's ice and white containers. Not just a bucket, by the way. That will work for a while, but if you use a bucket, look inside and watch how your minnows gather therein. 90% will be at the bottom 20% of the bucket.

SHH: I want you to use a rectangular-shaped cooler, and it could be the cheapest form of Styrofoam junk you ever saw. Get one that is big enough to hold as much water as the standard five — gallon bucket. But note: the bait that you have in it will stay in that same 20% of the bottom of the container, and because it is nearly twice as long and half as high as the bucket, the bait will have nearly two times as much space to swim around in.

The color white will, of course, throw off heat and keep the water as cool as possible, and adding ice from time to time will help even more. Periodically though, do dip out small containers of water off the top of your bait carrier and add in new water. The water you add will be too warm but it will also have lots more life giving oxygen in it. Add a few more ice cubes to offset this.

Some baitfish will require more care than others but if you want good, fresh bait all day, try the above combination to give you the best opportunity.

SHH: Other methods of helping keep bait alive include the use of a portable bubbler. Some are cheap and others rather costly. Generally speaking, $5-10 should get you what you want. Make certain it isn't too noisy because the sound could make you nuts. Another method involves the placement of small gray oxygen-containing tablets in the water every now and then.

SHRIMP/CRAWFISH: From one end of the states to the other, shrimp are among the favorite treats for kids and grownups, and here is where we share our pleasure with fish. I've even used cooked shrimp for bait in Norway, and fishing off a pier at Oslo, produced a nice catch of "fleunder" that way. Fish love to eat shrimp as much as

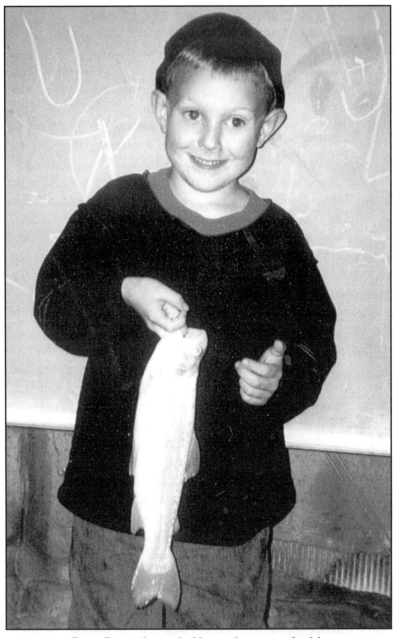

*Dave Pacovsky probably used a worm for his
first ever Palomino trout at McDade State Park, Pennsylvania.*

*Here's Ward Sandler
of Flagtown, New Jersey,
holding onto a bait fish for dear life
on his first fishing trip ever.*

we do, and if alive, the bigger fish are often ready to pounce.

The freshwater equivalent of shrimp is called crawfish/crayfish, and these make wonderful live baits. Of course if you are near Louisiana, someone might rip you off and put your "bait" into some good old "Crawfish pie!"

EELS: A live eel is not for the faint of heart but since the goal is to tell you what you can use, now or another day later on, it is important to tell you about live eel fishing. A live eel is not for me, but fish certainly do enjoy eating the slimy critters. I caught three striped bass from 10-15 pounds one evening in Sandy Hook Bay, New Jersey, using the very same little half-dead eel. It stayed on through three different bites and catches before I finally removed it from the hook.

WORMS: Freshwater or salt, after live fish, worms may make up the second most natural form of bait available, and my guess is that more fish are caught on worms than on anything else. In saltwater, a variety of worms are available ranging from sand to blood to tape. Freshwater fish have an even greater assortment of worms to go after. The standard night crawler or baby night crawler leads the list. But "glass" (they are very brittle), garden hackle or red worms are everywhere. Then add in the critters that eventually grow into something else like butter worms, mealworms, etc., and you have quite an assortment.

CHAPTER 3

Chumming
In Freshwater

Saltwater anglers all know the value of chumming, but most sweetwater guys have no clue how good it can be. Over the years, I have found that a combination of double anchoring and chumming has dramatically improved my catch total.

Chumming involves dropping material overboard around your boat to attract fish. The "freebies" often make up the difference between catching a fish or two and catching a dozen fish or two!

If you are after good-sized fish, don't chum with a sunken container on a rope. The filled container might leach out particles of food to fish in your area, but the line that is attached to the chum pot is a tangle attractor. Any good-sized fish that is worth anything can and will find the dangling line and wrap your fishing line around it a few times. Yes, cat-fishermen love to hang a burlap sack filled with the nastiest smelling masses of mush they can find down at bottom. But they are using very heavy fishing line and if a 20-pound channel catfish wraps around the sack rope, heavy fishing line has at least a chance at helping you land your prey. Other than when using very heavy line though, avoid a chum bag or pot, please.

Depending on what you are after, your freshwater chum could be corn kernels, dough or bread, cooked cornmeal, rice, or bits of fish. I cut up leftover shiners or herring and drop them overboard. Anyone who ever played marbles can remember how they put the marble between their thumbnail and the top joint of their "pointer" finger and then flicked the marble out with the thumb. Well, this style can be successfully used to launch a piece of fish out anywhere from 10 to 50 feet, depending on wind, weight of the chum, and launching power of your mighty thumb.

I've cleaned fish later in the day that had dozens of chunks of my chum in their bellies. I've also observed some that I was reeling up which were literally throwing up a bunch of my chunks.

Freshwater chumming? Especially if you are fishing on anchor, it really works. It also works well if fishing from a pier.

British carp experts carry an assortment of devices that permit them to throw chum way out. Most "carpers" fish from shore instead of from a boat. They may launch their "freebies" with a slingshot (this is quite illegal in much of the United States though, so be certain that you are doing something legal before trying it). Others use a long aluminum rod with a hollowed out top end. They fill the top with ground baits, flavored maize, etc., and, holding the skinny end in one hand, whip the mass out from the top as far as they can. With enough experience, they can lay out a barrage of chum that covers the area they will fish.

CHAPTER 4

Tackle

The "Can Man" Way

We sophisticates like to think that there is really only way to catch fish — via the use of a rod and reel combination. However, if you have ever been on vacation at any of the tropical islands, you have undoubtedly seen barefoot anglers fishing from the rocks or piers who were catching a nice assortment of warm water fish, with no rod and reel at all. The more typical gear used is a coffee can or such as a container, something to wrap hundreds of feet of monofilament line around. The business end of the line has a rock (or if affluent enough an angler, maybe a sinker) with one or two hooks attached to the line.

If you watch carefully, you will see these fishermen swing the weight around and around their head and throw their baited hooks out to sea. And they get far, far out, by simply holding the can top or bottom open end out. The line melts off the can and the baited hooks are deposited a long distance away. And if they do get a bite, which occurs often, the angler pulls back on the line and then winds the line in by hand around the can until the fish can be lifted up. So, rod and reel? Not obligatory, but it sure helps.

Pole Fishin'

Some locals also like to catch their fish on long, lightweight poles with line attached up at the top. No, no reels, just the pole itself, maybe ten or even 20 feet long. I've seen people in Italy holding such rods and they seemed to be even longer than 20 feet. My guess is that they are collapsible into themselves to make carrying easier. As a kid we would often go fishing by cutting a long live branch from a tree and trim away the leaves. This "fishing pole" may have been rustic to say the least, but we caught fish on it anyway. Later on, the use of a cane or bamboo pole — 10-15 feet in length would work well and in fact, cannot be beaten as a beginner outfit for a youngster. Whether using a cane pole at a "pay pond" or while standing at the end of a pier, this style is simplicity itself. The more expensive cane poles come in two to three sections with lightweight ferrules that allow you to attach them to make a single long pole.

Reel Fishing

REVOLVING SPOOL REELS: Once upon a time, the typical reel contained black braided nylon or maybe white Dacron line, and the line was brought up onto the reel from the bottom of the lake or ocean by the turning of a handle. The line would be released, on the other hand, by using a weight that turns the spool of the reel around backwards, letting the line go out.

Every reel, leastwise until the 50's, worked the same way, more or less. A spool held the line and a handle brought it in. Casting out would involve the spool going backwards. This required extreme expertise in casting and many an angler would foul up their line, big time, as they tried to cast the line out and clumsily created a tangle instead, commonly called a "back-lash," or birds nest.

The basic reel was one variation or another, the same deal. The spool was big or small, held heavy or light line, and had to revolve to release line. This could have been a "bait-casting" reel (smaller), a "fly reel" (used in fly fishing), or the larger ocean going "conventional" reel. Again, turn the handle and take in the line, or open the lever and release the line — controlling it so that the

Level-wind bait-casting reel. (UPSIDE DOWN!!)

spool didn't revolve so fast that it "back-lashed."

LEVEL-WIND REELS: So-called "Level-wind" reels go way back. The basic idea of this device is to eliminate the need to control the intake of line onto the reel with the use of your fingers. The typical conventional reel involves the turning of a handle and the intake of line. With most reels, one has to guide the line back and forth on the spool so that line doesn't all pile up on one side or the other of the spool. When a reel is properly filled with line, it ends about 1/8 of an inch below the top of the spool to allow an angler to reel in line a bit clumsily but still be able to get it all in. Some excited newcomers might crank in as fast as they could but not realize that they have to push line from one side of the spool to the other with their fingers.

"Level-wind" reels have a built in device that allows an angler to simply turn the crank and this control mechanism will retrieve the line back and forth onto the reel so that it winds it in level!

Just about all of the smaller bait-casting model reels are built with this level-wind feature and even some of the bigger and more expensive saltwater models have such mess-saving features.

FAST/SLOW RETRIEVE REELS: Conventional or spinning, some reels put line onto their spools far quicker than others. To turn a handle in a complete circle can bring anywhere from one revolution of the spool to as many as five or even six turns. Fly reels usually only bring one revolution per turn, but some of the bigger far offshore reels (like the Penn International Series) can drag great gobs of line in with one turn. This can be very important when fighting a large fish and the fish decides to charge the boat.

Fixed-spool spin-cast or spinning reels can also bring in little or lots of line, depending on how fast a retrieve you might want to achieve.

FIXED SPOOL REELS: The advent of spin-cast and spinning reels created an entire New World for all fishermen clear across the land. Tangles of line caused by sloppy casting would become a thing of the past (other than for the angler who was so masochistic that he still needed to have ten conventional reels in his arsenal). Spinning reels eventually found their own niche and fishermen found that they might still need to have a few conventional reels, but when spin-cast or spinning appeared in the 50's, things got lots better!

A "Spin-cast" reel has a "closed face," meaning that the line is wound onto the spool through an opening in a metal or plastic cover that fits over the reel itself. You can prepare to cast your line out with such a reel by the mere touching of a button that allows line to be thrown out a great distance. "Closed face" reels were what everyone in the southern part of the United States used, and they still are very popular in such areas.

But "Open faced" spinning reels eventually appeared and replaced most of the other kind. The main reason the "open face" reel is more popular is because you can see your line through its "open face" — duh!

I remember using a closed face reel one day as I was fighting a big carp and the fish took off lots of line in its battle to achieve freedom, and then, suddenly, line could no longer go out. The fish had pulled off all the line and I had reached the knot, without knowing it because I couldn't see into the reel. My friend and I

An Open-faced spinning reel.

hopped into our docked boat and followed the fish downstream as I gained line back. Eventually, I landed and released the 12-pounder, but swore off the use of spin-cast reels forever afterwards.

Spinning reels might be a poor choice of names because the reel doesn't spin but the line itself spins off of a fixed spool. Much greater distance can usually be achieved by casting such spinning reels and tangles are few, if ever. Remember, with conventional, the spool revolves and with spinning, the line melts off of a fixed spool. The weight of your lure or sinker, combined with the whippiness of your rod, mixed with your own skill, determines just how far you can cast with a fixed spool reel.

Just as an aside, most reels, fly, conventional, spinning, etc., are made for right-handed anglers. Yes, some companies do make reels that a port-sider can use, but righties still rule the world. (Yes, I'm left-handed, wanna' make something out of it?). Penn Reels has made reels specifically for lefthanders for as many years as I have been an angler, but when spinning reels came out, a new deal altogether was established, and I got confused!

The real spinning guys use a reel that is fixed to the rod from below, with open face pointed outward. Conventional reel anglers have their reel on top of the rod. They release line and are always looking at the top of their reel as line runs out. They turn the handle with right or left hand, based on what style it is.

Spinning guys though, originally, only could reel in with their left hand. Hey, not bad, I thought, but I was wrong. The idea was to cast out by holding the rod and reel in their power arm (right) and cast out. When bait or lure hit the water, the rod was still in their right hand, and they could immediately start the retrieve with their left hand. This got them to quickly engage the lure and start it back in with no delay. But for me, no one taught me, and instead, I would cast left-handed, transfer the rod then to my right hand, and then start to reel in lefty.

I always thought that I was using a left-handed reel but instead, I was cranking with what was a so-called righty outfit. Nowadays the reel manufacturers have made their reels with a device that allows them to change the handle so that it could be either left or right-hand retrieve. To this day though, I still do it wrong, so go shoot me. I reel with the "wrong hand," my left one, while using a righty reel. (If this confused rather than helped you, honestly, it doesn't matter, I've been fishing all wrong for 50+ years so don't tell anyone about me and I won't let them know that you are wrong also, okay?)

FLY REELS: This one is so complicated that we will talk about the entire topic of fly fishing all at one time in a few pages.

"Drag"

And while we are on the subject of reels, let's talk about the "drag" which allows line to be taken off of a reel if a fish pulls hard enough. You see, if your reel's drag isn't adjusted properly, a big fish could snap your line. So be it conventional or spinning, each reel has an adjustment device of sorts that controls line release,

An assortment of quality fly reels.

other than for casting. Ask your tackle dealer to explain it if need be, or simply read the directions that come with the new reel.

Only people who are after very small fish with very heavy line need not worry about this problem. But even an angler who is seeking a one pound fish might get surprised by a beast, and with tightened drag, snap! often results.

Fly fishermen create a drag when a big fish is running off line by holding a finger on the reverse revolving reel spool, if the fly reel isn't equipped with a true drag. But every other reel on the market has a lever or knob that can be turned this way to make line easy to be removed, and that way to tighten it up. Learn your reels drag adjustment well, a very important lesson!

Oil

SHH: Hey, not really a top secret, but just in case you didn't think about it, make sure you have reel oil with you whenever you go fishing. In fact, most of the better reels come with a little tube of oil tucked right into the box the reel was packaged in. Follow the instructions contained in the carton and you should get a long life of use out of every reel you buy. If you don't fish often, make certain to oil after a long delay before you head out again.

Fishing Poles — The Reel's Partner

FLY RODS: A fly rod is not very complicated. It is anywhere from long to longer, and nearly always comes in several parts. Frankly, I've never seen one that was one piece, and maybe that's because fly rod anglers really like to travel and rods that are joined by ferrules make packing easy to do. Most such rods are made with three or four joints and pack down to as little as a two or three foot package. Fit into a cloth container, or metal tube, some can even be squeezed into a suitcase.

Fly rod guys usually dress prettier than most of us, and wear gear with names like Orvis, Abercrombie & Fitch, instead of Penn and the like.

Vests? Oh yeah, with pockets for tweezers, forceps, hemostats, nail clippers, fly line oil, leaders, fly containers, sinkers, and heaven forbid, bait, plus maybe a barometer, and a fathometer (okay, I exaggerate). Add extra leaders and tippet material, and fly floatant. Throw in polarized sunglasses, a brimmed hat, and felt soled waders with sufficient traction to let you walk without mimicking the famous "Luftglass Green Rock Flop."

Most fly rods are made out of glass, although a few are still produced out of split bamboo. I'm not much of a fly rodder so I turned to my friend, Joe Perrone, a former licensed fly rod instructor on some of the fabled trout streams of Upstate New York for more details on this topic. Therefore, let's hear from him now.

What Is Fly Fishing
And What Do I Need To Get Started?
Contributed by Joe Perrone

Fly fishing need not cost a fortune. However, there are basic equipment requirements that must be met. There are also concepts that need to be understood in order to get started.

Let's begin with the activity itself. What exactly is fly fishing? For starters, it is not bait fishing. It is a method of fishing for trout (and more recently, for other fish, even way out in the ocean) that employs imitations of insects (or baitfish) using bits of feathers, fur and other materials tied onto a hook. But the major difference is in the line itself. In spin fishing, or bait casting, the weight of the lure or bait pulls the line off the spool as a cast is made and the lure is delivered to the target. In fly fishing, it is the weight of the line that propels the nearly weightless fly to the target.

FLY LINES: There are two major types of fly lines: floating (the most commonly used type) and sinking (slow, fast or intermediate sink). There are two types of floating lines: double taper and weight forward.

A double taper line is approximately 30-35 yards long, with identical 10-foot tapered sections on each end. The taper transmits energy gradually to the tip, allowing for precise, delicate presentations, and the "double" aspect of the line allows for reversing the line when one end becomes worn out.

A weight forward line is approximately the same length, but consists of a narrower diameter "running" line of about 65 feet in length, which gradually tapers to a wider "head" of approximately 20 feet, followed by a shorter tapered end of about six feet. The effect is somewhat like casting a rock with a string. Longer casts are definitely easier to make, but delicate presentation becomes a bit less predictable. In addition, once the weight forward end of the line becomes worn, the fly line is useless.

Fly lines come in many weights. For trout fishing, the general range is between weights 4, 5 and 6, with a 5-weight being the preferred line for a beginner. A double-taper, 5-weight, floating line would be represented as DT-5-F, and so on.

FLY RODS: Okay, so now you've selected a line. What about the rod? Fly rods vary considerably in design, material and cost. Most fly rods are manufactured either of fiberglass or graphite, with the latter being preferred. It is possible to purchase fly rods that cost as little as fifty dollars or as much as five hundred dollars, but all of them will cast a fly line adequately. Rest assured, whichever rod you select, it will perform "light years" ahead of any rod at any price available twenty years ago.

The way a rod flexes and where it flexes are all variables that should be considered in making a purchase. Some rods are soft, some are medium, and some are stiff. In addition, where the rod flexes makes a difference in its casting characteristic. A rod that bends primarily in the tip is a fast action while a rod that bends uniformly throughout its length is termed parabolic. A rod that bends in the first 40 per cent would be medium action, and is the preferred type for a beginner.

REELS: A fly reel has often been described as "nothing more than a device for storing line." In actuality, this is pretty close to accurate when describing a trout fly reel. Since small fish are very often played with the fly line "in hand," the reel serves primarily as a storage device. However, when fighting larger fish, a drag is generally of some importance. For most beginners, a simple click drag is sufficient. This is known as a pawl and sprocket design, with drag being supplied by a simple spring against the "clicker." In addition, there are fly reels available with disc drags, made of various materials such as cork, etc. These reels can cost upwards of one hundred dollars.

Most fly reels are "single action," with 1:1 gear ratios,

and these are the most commonly used fly reels for fly fishing. Saltwater fly fishing requires a reel with more drag and a higher gear ratio. These can be quite pricey.

TERMINAL TACKLE: Terminal tackle refers to the terminus or end of the line, and includes leaders, flies, fly floatant, fly boxes, ad nauseum. A leader is a piece of monofilament, usually tapered, attached to the end of the fly line and to the fly at the other. Most commercially manufactured trout leaders are either 7½' or 9' in length, and have a tippet section designated according to its diameter. The tippet is the last 30 inches or so of the leader. It is to this material that the fly is attached.

Leaders are referred to in increments of X, such as 4X, 5X, 6X, etc. with the higher number being finer in diameter than the lower X number. This system of identifying tippets was arrived at as an easier way than remembering diameters in thousands of an inch. It follows a rule called "the rule of 11." Put quite simply, if one subtracts the "X" number," e.g. 5X from the number 11, the result is 6, or .006" in diameter. Therefore, a 3X tippet is .008" in diameter, or the result of subtracting the 3(X) from 11.

For purposes of simplifying this subject even more, use leaders of nine feet, with a tippet of 4X or 5X for most of your dry fly fishing, and leaders of seven and a half feet, with a tippet of 3X or 4X for most of your nymph or streamer fishing.

NYMPHS, STREAMERS AND FLIES? WHAT ARE THEY?: Relax. Nymphs are the imitation of the substage of the mayfly, and streamers imitate baitfish. As for "flies," there are literally thousands of fly patterns, "wet" or "dry," but suffice it to say that equipped with a dozen or so, the average fly fisherman can expect to catch fish.

A "wet" fly is one designed to sink and a "dry" floats. Each is created to match the appearance of a local insect.

IN CONCLUSION: A basic fly fishing outfit, suitable for small fish, would be an eight-foot graphite rod matched to a double-taper, 5-weight line, with a single-action reel. Naturally we have only touched the surface of fly fishing here. However, hopefully, we have "wetted" your appetite sufficiently for you to want to get started.

In any case, it is suggested that you visit your library or local fly shop, where you will be able to obtain books and magazines, and learn more about this wonderful form of fishing. And for certain, join "Trout Unlimited" if you have a local chapter to get more inside information.

BAIT CASTING RODS: Bait casting rods used to come in very short lengths, mostly one piece, but some were two section as well. They went anywhere from five to six feet long and were used in connection with little slow revolving reels that freshwater anglers developed great expertise with. We all had one of two of them back in the 40's and 50's and as noted earlier, black braided line was on the reel.

The bait casting rods have little guides along their way that lead up to a tip-top which makes for a simple outfit. But the bait casting outfits of old really were extremely limited. Only the pros really could get more than fifty feet out on a cast, regardless of what kind of lure they were trying to throw. And the term "backlash" may have been invented in connection with these difficult to use reels.

And then a new generation of bait casting rods was invented, maybe in the 80's or so. These were anywhere from 7 to even 10 feet long, and many were one piece deals. The typical rod now used on most of the large lake charter boats in America is this stick. It can bend over into a "U" shape while doing battle with a big salmon or even a halibut up Alaska way, and still best the beast. Of course such a rod must be matched with a reel, a reel that holds hundreds of yards of line.

So-called "Noodle-rods" appeared in the 90's, and they are tailor-made to handle big fish in small water. I think that more are made to be matched with spinning reels, but I'm sticking them

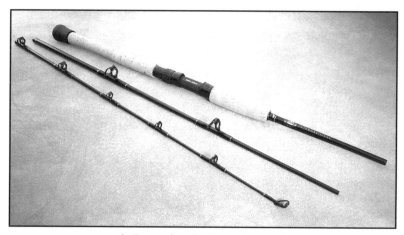

A three-piece bait-casting rod.

with bait casting ones if you don't mind. The bottom line is that they are extremely long, maybe 12-14 feet even, and are incredibly flexible, thus the name "noodle." They are built to take the shock of a big fish like river salmon or steelhead running line out. My guess is that carp anglers in the United Kingdom have taken to this kind of stick as well to increase sport.

SPINNING OR SPIN-CAST RODS: A spinning rod is one that has a huge guide down closest to the reel, with guides up the length of the pole that diminish in diameter until you reach the tiptop. The purpose of this is to allow the line to be released off the reel with the quickest of motion as it "spins" out. The decreasing opening of the successive guides funnel the line out in balance, allowing an angler to really get controlled distance on a cast. Whatever you do though, don't use a little ultra-lite outfit in the ocean, or even in a big lake while after large fish, unless you have chartered the boat all to yourself, or maybe own it! And the silliest thing you might see is a guy holding a 12-foot surf spinning rod way out in front of him on a crowded headboat. These rods are nearly impossible to use while fishing from a party or charter boat, thus the name "surf rod," got it?

Most "spin-cast" rods are made with their guides not being as wide near the reel and they don't taper down as much either. (But

*Use a surf rod in the surf like Ann Buonocure
of New York City did when she caught her first ever striped bass
(25.2 pounds) from the sands of Cape Cod.*

because of this, maybe, they don't seem to cast lures or bait as far out either.)

CONVENTIONAL RODS: Conventional rods come in a variety of diameters and lengths, depending on what kind of fishing you intend to do. For the most part, they are all used in saltwater, and are made to bring fish up from pretty deep water. Most shallow water fishing is done with spinning or the newer bait casting reels. Most are one-piece but a few are still produced in two sections. Your little angler can use a five-footer, but you too can put it to good use while fishing from a rowboat or even a charter craft. 99% of all of these rods are made out of fiberglass now. For typical boat fishing, go with a 6 to 8 foot rod.

Some conventional rods are made in 10-12 foot lengths. These are "surf rods," intended to be used for throwing heavy lures or sinkers out from the beach. I've seen guys on board party boats that use them but the rod is far too long for the task at hand and is really not what you want. In fact, surf rods create a mess because they are too tough to move with on a crowded boat and tangle often. However, they do have a time and a place. I saw guys with 15 footers in Hawaii who needed to get way out, and without the whippy length, they couldn't do it.

PACK RODS: I own a few rods that come in many sections and fit into little plastic tubes. Truth be known, most are too whippy to handle anything big, but I fished one in Denmark once on a party boat and managed to catch a mess of school codfish on it. When put together, a pack rod usually stretches out to six feet in length. When going on vacation, if you don't want to drag a monster sized hard plastic container with you that you could wait a lifetime for at the airline conveyor belt, this little pack rod can still work out.

Some people call very whippy rods "fast" and stiffer poles "slow" action. Simple enough, the skinny stick whips fast and the heavyweight model doesn't.

The Good With The Bad

We talked about graphite rods up in the fly rod section, and many of the better sticks are now made out of this material, or at least graphite composite, for every style rod. These rods are usually stronger, lighter, and in most ways, better — but —

SHH: They have been known to conduct electricity. Don't get me wrong, I have a few and love them, but if an electric storm were to occur, Manny is off the water, pronto. I don't want to be Ben Franklin out there with lightning popping around, with a graphite rod in hand, no-sir-ree.

And here I am again on this subject, exactly three days after writing the above paragraph with a first-hand report. I have owned two graphite spinning rods for upwards of ten years and never had an experience worth noting about them, other then, maybe, to say that both rods perform very well. Well-known companies manufacture each. One is an ultra lite and the other is stiff, something I use for deepwater lake fishing.

Okay, exactly three days after putting the information down about the deal with graphite and electric storms, I was on the water with my friend in a very calm, cloudy day. There was no report of "weather" to come. And the fish were biting well. We had scored maybe 20 trout between us and expected more, but the air got kind of heavy. It "felt like" rain, if you know what I mean. Forgetting about it, I picked up a graphite rod and got a shock in my hand.

Paying no never mind to it, thinking I must have been mistaken, I disregarded it and put the rod down again. This took place two more times, with a little "zap" hitting my hand as I lifted the rod just where the glass goes into the butt of the rod. AND THEN THE RAIN BEGAN!

No, we were not whacked with lightning, thank goodness. We took our lines in and headed back for the barn as the rain came down. Call graphite a conductor of electricity if you want, or think that "static electricity" was the culprit. All that I can tell you as that from now on, I will heed my own words very carefully and be super cautious.

CHAPTER 5

Balance

Everything has to work correctly together, your rod and reel, with proper line, as well as how to get the whole deal out there where the fish live (casting), so let's get into each of these three topics now.

Rod To Reel

We've talked about this a little already, but let's get more specific. Sure, you can put a fly reel on a five-foot stand-up tuna rod, but someone will throw you overboard because you look like an idiot! Matching the rod to the reel is something you may need help with. But one very simple way to do this is to mount the basic kind of reel on the basic type of rod, and then try to balance it all.

Try this — say a six-foot medium-action spinning rod with a regular sized Penn spinning reel. Put the reel on the rod, tighten it up, and then try to balance the rod on two fingers. If the whole outfit jiggles up and down somewhere near where the reel is mounted, you have gotten a combination that is in proper balance. If the rod tip dips down to the ground at this time, the rod is too heavy. If the rod butt looks like a divining rod, the reel is far too heavy for the rod. Of course the easiest way to get a rod and reel in balance is to ask the guy behind the counter in the tackle store for help. Do not, though, take his or her advice if they themselves aren't true fishermen.

Line To Reel

It's a given that "enough" line has to be on your reel to be able to cast efficiently as well as retrieve line as quickly as you can. Most of the pros feel that whatever the kind of reel, it should be filled to within an eighth or a quarter of an inch from the top edge of the spool. "Level-wind" reels can get more line than others, but still shouldn't be loaded to the very maximum range. Regular reels in particular cannot be filled to brimming because as you reel in, you may not retrieve it carefully enough and you could pile too much line in one spot, jamming the reel and making it impossible to get any more in.

This, by the way, usually coincides with a few things — a big audience and a bigger yet fish. It is both embarrassing and frustrating to have a beast of a fish on your hook, maybe 25 feet away, and then you jammed the line onto one side of the reel making it impossible to get any more line in. At this point, you should create a diversion so that others will not see you put the rod down and take the line in hand over hand to try and get the fish into the boat. Try to shout something like "fire" to make them look elsewhere!

"Backing" is line that is taken up onto your reel for a variety of reasons. If the spool holds an enormous amount of line, you may want to put some cheaper stuff on first that partially fills the reel. When a huge fish takes though, you may want a full spool of the same quality line that is attached to the hook. The only good reason for using "backing" at the bottom of the reel may be if you are a fly fisherman. "Fly line" is very heavy and unless you have a fly reel that holds lots and lots of fly line, you really want to put a bunch of plain mono on first. Fill the spool halfway and then add fly line. Make certain to tie an appropriate knot to get the fly line tightly onto the mono. Very specific contraptions are made to make this knot secure.

The general subject of balance of line to reel is simple but

"The art of casting."

sometimes complicated for beginners, so let me touch on this rather than bore you with too many details. Big reels equal big line, and little reels equal, on the other hand, light line. Simple? Sure, but let's take that a bit further out now. A spinning reel can be made with a "deep" or "shallow" spool, and for that matter, conventional, bait casting, and even fly reels come that way so before buying a reel, make sure how much line it can hold. Some even come with two different spools: shallow and deep. Check them out with the tackle store guy.

To help determine how much a reel can hold, the box should tell you. A freshwater reel could hold, for example, 125 yards of 10-pound test, 150 yards of eight, or 200 of six. Big oceangoing way offshore reels have line capacity that can boggle the mind. Some of the big gold reels that cost as much as a used car can handle 1,000 yards of stuff that is near-rope width, for tuna, blue marlin, etc. Whatever you do though, don't buy a reel that makes you convert from metric to plain English, unless you want to show off how smart you are.

Put line on a reel that balances with it. Don't put 50-pound line on a spinning reel, or 10-pound on a 4/0 ocean model. And while we are talking about line, let's go over the four or five basic kinds that are out as we start our next chapter.

Casting

Other than fly fishing, a subject all to itself, most casting is really pretty simple. Fly casting requires far more knowledge and practice so if you want to learn how to get your fuzzy-wuzzy flea out there to where trout or sailfish live, read separately about this skill. A half-hour of class or working with a guide should be considered to make sure you know how to do it right.

Otherwise, casting involves the two basic reel forms we have already talked about — fixed spool and revolving.

Fixed spool reels (spinning or spin-casting) are far easier. All you need to do is read the instructions that come with your reel. If it is a spin-cast, a button needs to be pushed to allow you to "open" the reel and release line. Spinning reels require you to either move the "bale" to an open position or pull a little triggering device that automatically opens it for you.

Either way, tangling is kept to a minimum with these reels. Once you know how to hold the line on your pointer finger to avoid dropping line, the next step is simple enough. With lure or sinker held a foot or two below the top of your rod, hold the rod straight up. Then bend your arm and wrist back a little bit, and fling it all out straight ahead of you.

This same basic style is followed when casting fixed spool reels, but more care is needed to avoid a backlash (tangle). To cast properly, you have to firmly hold your thumb on the spool as you prepare and then lift the thumb partially as you swing the rod out. Do this a dozen times in an open field or wherever you can find open water and you will get the idea. You may tangle a few times and you will probably release your finger too soon or too late once or twice as well. But soon enough, you will become expert enough to get it right.

CHAPTER 6

Types Of Line

#1 by far, is monofilament. Sure, different manufacturers produce this material in a variety of qualities, diameters, and colors. Owning maybe 20 freshwater spinning reels, I use the "K.I.S.S." method (keep it simple stupid), and therefore use two colors and weight measurements. If I see pink on a reel I know it's six-pound test. And the other half of my K.I.S.S. goes with eight-pound white. I don't really like any other color but pink or white and feel that I can handle nearly anything in sweetwater on six- or eight-pound test line. As for saltwater, again, white or pink but I go anywhere from 10-pound to 50-pound depending on what I am after and where I am fishing.

#2 — Non-stretch line. This really helps when fishing in deep water. It's super sensitive and you can feel a bite far better with such material. Typically, 20-pound non-stretch line is as skinny as most 8-pound mono so you can also get a lot more line onto a small reel. The big problem with such line is that if a fish is running drag off the spool and you get a digit in the way, they may call you four-finger Louie from then on. Well, maybe that's an exaggeration, but it really can cut if you aren't careful. I have a few fingers that have been sliced.

#3 — Wire. Wire line is used for trolling, almost exclusively. It clearly is the most dangerous because, after all, it is wire, so under no circumstances should a beginner ever use it unless a mate or captain is standing right alongside of you. Guys who troll in salt or freshwater use it when downrigger fishing. The only other way that I have seen wire in use is for conventional rod and reel fishing with bait in very deep water. Specifically, when you drift in 400 to 600 feet of water for tilefish, non-stretch wire will be very good. You will feel your bites and hold bottom better on a drift.

#4 — Fly/dacron/braided. Each has its own purpose and for the specific need, has its own place too. Other than fly line, though, most of you will never need the other lines.

#5 — Synthetic fluorocarbon lines have been produced that claim to be invisible in the water and lots of anglers now swear by the stuff. Maybe they cannot afford filling a reel with it, but at least they feel that their leaders should be made with such material.

CHAPTER 7

Freshwater Fishing

"Freshwater" may be a bit of a stretch. While some such water may be clean enough to allow you to dip a cup into it and take a good long drink, I regret that "fresh" may not be so terribly good for you because it may contain mercury, PCB's, and so on. So take the word FRESH-water loosely, and just consider it as water that has no salinity content, okay?

We will lump brackish water into the mix here, to make things easier. "Brackish water" is simply defined as water that contains both salt and freshwater. As freshwater rivers run downstream, sometimes water enters from a saltwater body and the long sections that contain both waters are what we call "brackish."

Lakes And Ponds

I never actually saw anything written that defined the difference between a lake and a pond, but my rule of thumb is simple enough. If it takes an Olympian to swim across, it's a lake. And if your cat can make it from one shore to the other, that's a pond. Of course the easy distinction is based on size, but I have also seen a spot that is labeled a "pond" which may require a gasoline-powered engine to maneuver from one end to the other.

As we get further into this chapter we will talk about what kind

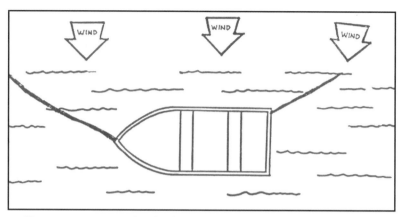

Boat appearance after both anchors are properly set in bottom.

of boat to use and where. Suffice it to say that the use of a canoe or small "Johnboat" is not wise on a large lake or reservoir. More on that later on.

DOUBLE-ANCHORING: If you ever pick up any of my other fishing books, you will see in each one that I really love to go fishing in a small boat. I "double-anchor" my boat, the *Gone Fishin' IV,* 99% of the times that I go fishing.

This is done to get your boat positioned in a way that allows you to get the best use of your space. If you set both anchors correctly, you can fish an entire side of your boat with multiple rods and hardly ever tangle up. You can also put a few rods on the other side of the boat.

Double-anchoring takes some time and energy away from the instant fishing that many anglers prefer to do. I virtually never approach a spot in stealth-like silence and cast lures to fish that are wildly attacking bait. Hell yes, I can feel my juices boiling even as I type this stuff, but it really doesn't occur too often, especially in freshwater. For sure, when I see hybrid bass chasing herring to the surface, and sea gulls swooping down to pick off dazed baitfish, I will switch to my electric motor and run silently to the area and then throw lures or bait in the area of the frothy water. But because I only get to do that three or four times yearly, let's instead discuss what I do just about every other time out.

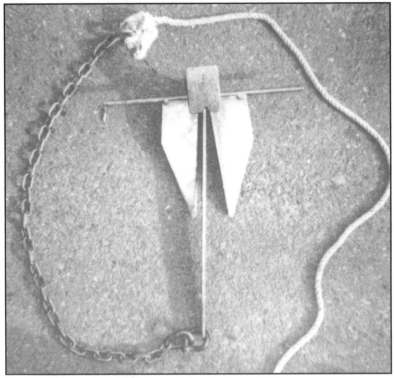

Danforth anchor, chain and line.

My boat contains two anchors. They are "Danforth" models, and each weighs four pounds. (Bigger boat = heavier anchor). The so-called "Danforth" has a long metal pole with two pointed "flukes" attached. These are shaped like your middle and pointer fingers, allowing the two "points" to dig into bottom. Attached to the anchor joint loop is a four-foot length of chain (heavy chain for bigger anchor, etc.), and at the loose end of the chain I tie on my anchor line. It should be 3/8-inch nylon line, not your mother's clothesline or that nasty yellow stuff that splinters with ease.

I buy my line in very long lengths and actually have 300 feet of it coiled in the front of my boat. If you have quality line, with no knots, it will hardly ever tangle, even at such long length.

SHH: Here, a word of caution. Do make sure that the "loose" end is not really "loose." If you drop the anchor in and back up and then

*watch the loose end disappear overboard, that means that you didn't
read the next few words. And the next few words are simple — TIE
THE LOOSE END ONTO THE BOW OF THE BOAT!*

A second Danforth with chain and long line can be found in the
back of my boat with, yes, its bitter end also tied securely to the
stern. You can pile 250 and even 300 feet of good line between the
last and middle seat of your boat, or maybe even behind the back
seat if you have room enough. Don't use one of those circular line
holders that you crank the line onto, other, perhaps, to hold it if you
know that you won't be fishing for a while. You see, you cannot
release line quickly enough off of such a spool during the anchoring process, — it needs to be loose!

All right, let's get anchored up. Presuming you are in an area
that you think is fishy (see "anchoring on a slope"), or have
actually seen fish on your scope below the boat, let's get busy. Be
certain that you know how much water is under you as well as how
deep it is where you want to set anchor #2 into. But first, make
sure your boat sits high enough off the water to withstand wind and
boat waves, or else don't even dream about double-anchoring.
Presuming you passed muster on that point, when you reach your
spot, slow the engine down and put it into neutral. You want to
wind up with a whole side of the boat facing straight into where the
wind is coming from, or where the weather report said it should be
blowing from. Don't ever put anchor number one in so that it
results in holding the bow straight into the wind, because you
won't anchor right that way.

Okay, boat now dead in the water, with engine running, drop #1
anchor over. Put the engine into very slow reverse, and release
line quickly overboard as the anchor heads to the bottom. Once it
reaches bottom, continue ever so slowly and after an extra 25-35
feet is out, gently grab hold of the line in an attempt to dig one of
the Danforth's blades into bottom. Release it now and continue to
back up. Do it again, holding the line tighter now in a more serious
try at digging in. If you are on "a slope," you should see on your
fish finder that you have reached shallower (or deeper) water by
now. If you are in 90 feet of water, I want you to get anchor #1 dug

in perfectly and still allow all of the 300 feet of line to go out.

Just before all of your line runs over the bow, put the boat into neutral. (It may be easier to have a friend in the bow, but you may also wind up with them catching more fish than you so let this factor into your decision on company or not.) As you go into neutral, drop stern anchor #2 over the side. Once it hits bottom, get to the bow and start to slowly pull on the bow line while holding the stern line loosely up forward with you while wrapped around a leg (maybe you shudda' had a buddy for the first few times to make it easier). Okay, start pulling the front of the boat to where the bow anchor is secured all at the same time as you release line #2 out the stern. After 25-35 feet, stomp on the stern line and try to get it dug in, and then release it and pull another 25-35 feet in from the bow. Repeat this until the stern anchor is tightly into bottom and each line has vibrated. The vibration translates into a secure anchorage.

Your intent is to start fishing once both anchors are at least 50+ feet away from each end of the boat. This will allow you to fish in comfort and still be able to fight a fish that tries to swim around the boat. Thus secured, you can go over or under the anchor with your rod and come up on the other side of the boat to continue to do battle.

Perhaps the main reason that people fish with one anchor, at least in my opinion, is that they don't have another one! Of course that is not true, because most people really don't know better. Unless you are in a large crowd of boats or it's too dangerous to set two anchors, I find the use of just one to be a big mistake. You see, if any manner of wind is blowing, your boat will flop back and forth in the wind and if you have more than one fishing line out, they will all tangle with the swing of the boat.

SINGLE, ON A "BRIDLE:" Okay, you forgot to bring a second anchor, or, heaven forbid, you got one so badly stuck in bottom when you tried to move to another place in the lake that you had to cut your line and now you only have one left. Since you probably don't want to go home yet, improvise!

Get your remaining anchor set up at the front end of your boat and tie on a separate 15 to 20 feet length of line from the stern. Put a loop in your main anchor line after it is adequately dug into bottom and tie the stern line in at the loop. If any kind of wind is blowing at all, the boat will settle into what is sometimes called a "bridle." An upside down Y will form in the line. If you have the same distance between the stern and bow cleats, you will see that the boat has the upside down point of the Y slightly underwater, and your boat is now sitting with one side facing upwind and the other downwind. (See illustration on page 55.)

DRIFTING: Again, a view from yours truly. The reason that fishermen drift is because they don't have any anchors. And, of course, that is not true, but I like saying it anyway!

In certain areas of saltwater, as you will read later, drifting in wind or current is done 99% of the time, and often, with great success. And yes, you can drift in a lake too, but you lose nearly all of your control that way. Random movement caused by increasing or decreasing, or worse yet, changing wind, will flop your boat around and around and wreak havoc if multiple rods are used.

Sure, if you find fish on top and quietly motor over and let the boat drift along with feeding fish, by all means, go for it; that will really work. But drifting and soaking bait will not be as productive as fishing on anchor in the manner discussed.

There are some anglers who like to drift in deep water, bouncing bottom with either bait or jig, and while they often catch fish, more often they catch the biggest kinds of tree stumps imaginable. I love to watch such boats with angler standing, pumping feverishly with his rod, and the monster fish he is trying to pump into the boat is really "Moby Tree" holding itself tightly to the bottom! And, giggle, giggle, I love watching those guys, but if they are very big, I carefully avoid them seeing me laugh.

TROLLING: Separate books have been written that were devoted mostly to the very fine art of trolling. "Trolling," simply, means that your boat is underway while you are fishing. I have "trolled" lures or live bait behind my boat while rowing, and caught fish that way. And, of course, the use of an electric motor too can be very productive because you have the opportunity of dragging bait or lure over water that you know holds fish, and if you can do this at a specific depth, that really is a way to score.

Let's say that you feel that the fish are swimming 10 feet down, and you are using an electric motor, or a gasoline one that you can really slow down to a crawl. The use of a 1½ to 2 ounce egg-shaped sinker may be quite productive. Run your line through the egg sinker and secure it with a clinch knot to a barrel swivel. Tie a 2-4 foot length of mono to the other end of the swivel and add your hook. Bait the hook and drop the whole deal down, say 15 feet or so if you want to troll 10 feet down. Engage the engine (or start to row), and the line will lift a little and you will be pulling it in a controlled movement.

By the way, do make sure you loosen the drag on your reel or prepare to have your line broken if a big fish hits. Yes, you can secure the rod in a rod holder, and this is highly recommended, but if the drag wasn't loosened, you may get your rod broken instead of the line!

Since this book is for beginners, I will not tell you much about the use of what are called "downriggers," other than to let you know that once you obtain expertise, it would be a good idea to add a down-rigger to each side of your boat. The real serious guys who troll have as many as four or even six of these contraptions on their boats.

Outrigger fishing is yet another style used in the ocean and at times, in the Great Lakes. Not at all simple, it involves the rigging of long poles that protrude out from each side of the boat. A pulley system gets your lines clipped to a point way out on each pole and this allows you to fish two lines well apart from any other line. When you get a bite, the "clip" (often something as simple as a kind of a clothespin) will release and your line will drop back, allowing you to fight your fish.

The fellows who are most knowledgeable in big hunks of freshwater also use a different style, called "Planer Board" fishing, and I won't even begin to try to explain this to you. But if you hit one of the Great Lakes for trout or salmon, you may find that this is another method. And if you develop enough skill doing it yourself, that will be the time that you should sit down and write your own book. I have no such skill and don't want to learn! With but a very few exceptions, I hardly ever do well while trolling, and generally find it to be as boring as watching a tree grow out my window. Yeah, when a squirrel or bird shows up, that could be interesting, but for the most part, trolling equals YAWN. I almost would rather be back at work with a tie around my neck — note, almost.

Rivers And Streams

A moving body of water is often both smaller in size and more dangerous, so here again, be absolutely certain that your boat is big enough for the task. A boat with low sides can easily be rolled over in current if you slip or worse, if you stand to fight a fish and bending over to net it, a gust of wind grabs hold and now you are wet!

DOUBLE-ANCHORING: Double anchoring is much easier in moving water, but can be an awful pain in the tail if a strong wind is blowing upstream. However, in most instances, the Danforth discussed above will work, but some fishermen prefer what is called a "River Anchor." This doesn't have a swinging blade but instead has groves that will grab bottom and hold you just fine. To double-anchor in current also involves setting anchors fore and aft, but here, the line faces straight upstream when you are properly set up. It really is easier to do this with a friend than by yourself because both anchors should be plopped over at the same time. If you are alone, put one down at the faster current end first and then quickly stick number two over. Don't try to dig either in before the other — that won't work. You want to release line in an even manner until both anchors get you settled and when both are in, release from one end or the other until a whole side of the boat faces upstream. You will be fishing the downstream side, of course.

BRIDLE-ANCHORING: Discussed above in the lake section, this system works even better in moving water than on a pond. Simply enough, stick an anchor in, put a loop in some of its slack line, and tie a length of stern line in so that an upside down Y shape is formed. Take in or release line at one end or the other so that the current positions the boat in a manner that gets a whole side of

JoAnn Keehnel of Washington State with her first king salmon
(23 pounds) caught in the Hoh River
with guide Mike Schmitz, Jr. of Forks, Washington.

the boat facing downcurrent while the other side faces upstream.
Fish the downstream side and you will find that you have much
more fishable space this way.

SHH: Of course, if you single anchor in current and it's your
boat, put the other dummy up in the front. Tell him/her that it's more
comfortable there and you gave them the choice space. Don't say that
fish face upcurrent and that 90% of the fish that bite will be on the
downcurrent end of the boat. Some of the "best" fishermen get to be

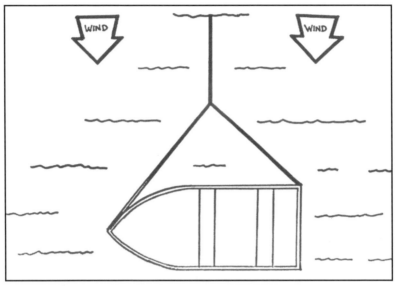

How the boat looks after setting up on the bridle.

"best" by taking the downcurrent end of a single anchored boat.

ANCHORING ON A SLOPE: Getting even more specific now about where to set your anchors, this system requires you to either know your water like the back of your hand, or to have a depth finder. Fish tend to look for any advantage that they can get. This applies in still water as well as moving. Since we are on the topic of moving water though, let's go with that. But do make sure to note that anchoring on a slope applies just as well on a lake as it does a river.

Your fish finder will mark depth changes. The bigger the change, the better your chance at big fish waiting above or below the drop-off for passing morsels. Sure, you can catch lots of fish on flat-bottomed water, but I would rather fish on a slope if I can find one.

ANCHORING ON OBSTRUCTIONS: Moving water will have downed trees and boulders stuck in bottom that act as obstructions. But they also act as holding sites for large fish that are waiting to pounce. I've seen this all too often on a small river. A big rock is out there, half-way to the other shore, and if you cast a little upstream of the rock and watch your line move just past it, as the baited hook or lure chugs around the rock, a waiting fish will lunge out and grab lunch.

These spots offer two key ingredients to feeding fish. First, a holding spot that breaks the current and allows them to rest. Second is a hiding place. As a baitfish, fly, etc., rolls around the rock and gets caught up further in the current, Mr. Fish is there waiting, and eat, he will.

Out in big water, this applies the very same way. If a big tree were nailed to the bottom in a winter storm (and in particular, is parallel to the current), count on a few fish hiding downstream of the heaviest wood. Any kind of food at all would be easy prey to the resting fish and this applies to everything from muskellunge to carp.

Pay Ponds And Waters

Talked about earlier, let's go deeper into these super bodies of water. A "pay pond" is your best guarantee of success. As a beginner, let's face it, you want to catch fish, or more importantly, you want grandma or junior to catch some. Therefore, start them out on stocked waters that charge a fee to fish.

I have seen channel catfish ponds near Galveston and Houston, Texas, and at a small lake in New Mexico that is filled with trout. Also I've seen a largemouth bass lake in Pennsylvania, a super place in New York State for trout, as well as a series of ponds in South Jersey that contain hybrid bass. And that doesn't even count Great Britain where anglers actually rent a "swim" (a spot along the bank of a pond) to fish for their beloved carp.

Just remember that every "pay" water has its own rules and regulations and the owner or manager sets the rules. Most places even say that applicable state regulations don't apply like size, bag or season limits. And many of them make it obligatory that you keep everything you catch — and pay for them by the pound. This can be very expensive!

Fishing Derbies

Derbies are run clear across America and probably exist on a worldwide basis. The basic theme is usually the same. An open

*Michael caught this snapper blue at the
2002 New London, Connecticut Fishing Derby.*

pond exists and it has fish in it. The local Police Benevolent
Association, or maybe the township Recreation Department or a
fraternal organization will bring anglers together to fish for free.
Prizes often are also awarded at such events and they range from
either the most, the biggest, or the smallest of fish.

Generally, food and cold beverages are provided and anglers may
also be given hooks, sinkers, and bait, at most of these derbies.
They usually are run for kids but some are for handicapped anglers
and still others exist for anyone who wants to participate. If you
want to start a person out, this may be the right place to begin
because there are usually volunteers on hand to assist. I've been at
many of them and had a blast at each and every one!

CHAPTER 8

How To
Hook 'Em

Freshwater anglers down in the southern part of America call it "Crossing their eyes!" Simply put, when a fish hits their lure or bait, they point the tip of the rod towards the water and slam the rod skyward, as quick and hard as they can. The idea is to take all slack out of the line and make sure a good, tight hook set occurs. So, "crossing their eyes" means that they slam a fish so hard that, more or less, its eyes were crossed by the force!

Simply put, when you are out fishing, nothing is more important than catching the fish that bites on your line. And a good "set" is key to success, with a few possible exceptions. Devotees of the so-called "Circle Hook" (a hook that is actually shaped into doggone near an entire circle, with but a small opening between ends) don't "set" at all. They get a bite, tighten their line until slack is out, and then reel as fast as they can. They feel that the hook will actually pull itself into the corner of the fish's mouth this way. On the other hand, they also think that they will not catch some of the fish if they try to slam the steel home with a strong set of the rod.

A significant problem occurs very often when an angler does everything right, sets, hooks the fish, and bang, they break their line. So setting isn't the only thing to know. One must also know his line's breaking point and adjust the drag on the reel so as to allow line to be released from the reel immediately after hooking the fish, just in case it is a critter that has sufficient weight to break a tight line.

Setting the hook — fresh or salt, limp or stiff rod, other than a concern for breaking your line on a big fish as just noted, it's pretty much all the same deal. A fish has your bait and you want to get the hook stuck into the fish. Point the rod at the fish, tighten up on slack, and quickly pull the rod tip high into the sky. If you took out all the loose line, chances are darn good that you will hook 'em!

Deep water fishing with light rods calls for yet more skill. When I am fishing in 100 feet of water and a lake trout bites at bottom, I wait until the fish starts to swim away with my bait before responding. Standing up, to give myself the best chance at getting any slack out of the line, I control a release of a few feet of extra line, all at the same time as I gently lift the rod up high. Then, as the fish moves further away I follow it with the rod tip until the top of the pole is actually in the water before slamming the rod as high as I possibly can. In this way, I usually score.

Brown and rainbow trout often will hit up. In fact, more than half of them do just that. With a float, you will notice that it flattens out when such a fish takes your bait. You will have to wait until the critter starts to swim away and then, at that time, reel in line, following its path, until you tighten up. Once you get a bend to the rod, that is when it's time to set, and not until then.

Guys who use the non-stretch lines have it much easier. They don't have to worry about their line not sticking a fish due to its natural stretch. But on the other hand, since such material doesn't stretch, one must be careful as to avoid snapping his line on a slam because non-stretch stuff doesn't give on a set.

Trolling involves a need to avoid setting a hook, however. More than likely, 95+% of fish that hit a trolled lure or bait will hook themselves. So you must avoid the natural tendency to take a trolling rod out of the rod holder and trying to set an already set hook. Because the fish has already gotten steel into its mouth past the barb, you stand a very good chance at creating a hole with a set and eventually, your hook will drop out during the fight. Soft mouthed fish like trout and salmon are particularly good at escaping in such moments.

So, to catch a fish is to set the rod, most of the time, but not while trolling and also not with a circle hook!

CHAPTER **9**

Hook Removal

"Two-pair" may be a winnable hand in poker, but "two-pair" is an essential element in successful fishing, especially if you are not out to kill a mess of fish. The two pairs that I am talking about are, 1) a pair of sharp scissors, and, 2) a pair of hemostats, preferably as long a set as you can buy.

If you want to take the fish home, neither one or two is as important, but both can help. However, if your goal is to release that particular fish that you caught (or nearly all of them), #'s 1 and 2 are both needed.

When you catch a fish and want to let it go, do not net it, if you can avoid doing so. You will remove protective slime and it could later get a skin problem. Instead, just lean over with the hemostat and remove the hook that is clearly showing in the mouth. And if the hook is buried way down inside, that is where "two-pair" number one, the pair of scissors, comes in. Lean over and cut the line without making the fish bleed and chances are better than 80-90% that the fish will head away in good health, with the hook certain to rust out in a short period of time. I have caught hundreds of healthy fish that had anywhere from one to five other hooks buried inside which were in one manner of disintegration or another.

CHAPTER 10

Clothing

Clothing For Cold Times

Yes, most of your mothers told you to wear mittens when it was cold out, with something to cover your head as well as nice, dry boots. So for you who already know that stuff, as well as the people who grew up where it never gets cold, let's expand your education on this a bit.

Freshwater fishing can take place on a warm sunny day in Texas, but lots of folks get out in the dead of winter in the north and still catch fish. And while we are on the subject of cold, think Alaska or maybe northern Canada!

Anyone with a teeny little brain already knows about dressing in layers, but what kind of layers work best? If you have room for it, always keep something with you that is waterproof to go over everything else you have or else your preparation will have gone for naught. And when we say "waterproof," that means that I want you to be able to get covered from head to toe with a covering that water or, heaven forbid, snow, cannot penetrate.

Start with a set of underwear, any set, really, and then, if the predictions call for it, add a layer of thermal underwear. Not always, but often, lightweight is all you need, providing the material will "breathe," and yet be skintight. I fished once on the Black

*Clothing for cold times. Ron Nadler (holding 17-inch salmon)
with 3-year old son Ethan during their first ice fishing trip
in upstate New York.*

River, a tributary out of Lake Ontario, while wearing two full sets
of thermals but since this book is for the beginner and not the rav-
ing idiot like I was that day, forget about it!

A heavy woolen shirt is usually next when it's cold out, and here
is a little personal secret that I will share with you. (And I'll repeat
it too when we talk about saltwater as a further reminder).

*SHH: Make sure the shirt has two breast pockets. And why, you
ask? Because something goes into each pocket. And one such
something is far less than two of 'em. I'm talking about those little
chemically treated warming baggies. If you have never seen them,
every tackle store above the Mason Dixon line carries them all winter, and lots of the big chains do as well. There are several companies
that make them and in winter, the difference between having two
working hand warmers in your pockets and not can spell the sepa-*

ration between wonderful comfort and being oh so cold.

Most of these little devices simply involve opening and removing the package inside and stuffing them into your pocket. Some require a little shaking. You may find that they provide too much warmth even if you have a tee shirt and thermal top under the woolen shirt. In such cases, wrap the baggie in a tissue or two and enjoy the body warming that follows.

We all too often worry about our ears, fingers and toes, honestly. With a warm chest (both sides, that's why I want you to have a two-pocket shirt on), that just about completes your anti-shiver costume.

They also make smaller versions that can fit into your boots in case you didn't remember to wear two sets of socks, or in the event it really is bitter cold out. As for your feet, with or without warmers, make sure you are in waterproof stuff. You may want to buy some boots that are a half size bigger than you generally wear, so that you can layer socks. A lightweight pair is worn under a heavier pair and some of these heavyweights come in thermal material to add to your pleasure.

Boots should be light enough to get out of if you are boat fishing, in case you get swamped. Heavy boots work like an anchor so avoid them while in a boat, but do make sure your footwear keeps you plenty warm.

Make certain that you have two hats with you which cover your ears. I have one that is fur-lined and has a strap that wraps around my neck and closes. The traditional Navy "watch cap" works great but some of them are so tight that five or six hours later your head feels like a squashed grapefruit.

Gloves are essential but in freshwater, you really cannot fish with them on so a couple of lightweight towels will be critically important here. Yes, two pair of gloves, especially if you are a guest in my boat and are required to pull that anchor a few times. Always have a dry pair at the ready while you travel from one spot to another.

I even have a scarf to wrap around my neck. If I look a little sissy boy on the water as you motor past me, chances are good to excellent that you may be near frozen as you point and laugh at the old guy who looks like the great woolly mammoth.

If you intend to wade a river or stream, you may need as many as three sets of rubber footwear. Neoprene makes the warmest and tightest bond, but can cost a ton of money. The more traditional green hip boots or waders may be all you need, if everything else underneath is warm enough.

I have a pair of pants that are fully lined which I wear over my thermals when it is really cold out. Make sure you buy these in a size larger than your regular pants because the lining will deny you the ability to close the top button otherwise. (And that's not a good thing at all!)

A loose fitting jacket should be in your closet to wear over your inner clothing and if it really is cold out, have a good sweater between the wool shirt and your jacket.

Top everything off with a good coverall set. If it has an attached hood, so much the better. Make absolutely certain that your coverall outfit is way, way big. In fact, bring your heavy jacket with you and try the coveralls on over the jacket in the store. If the zipper doesn't close with ease you may have to go up yet one more size. Yes, your arms and feet may appear to be buried in what now is really a polar bear looking set of garb but, hey, you do what you have to do to stay warm, OR ELSE — move to Florida! That may be my best suggestion of all to you.

Yet one more bit of advice here — layers don't work worth a damn if you don't tuck them into each other. Tee shirt into shorts, thermal top into bottom and thermal bottom bottoms into socks, etc. If you don't tuck each layer into the other, the whole deal goes out the window and you had better forget about fishing in the cold.

Assuming you have your car nearby, always keep an entire extra set of clothing with you, in case you either fall in, or get soaked 'cause you forgot the waterproof stuff.

Seriously, good quality "foul weather" gear can be worth its weight in gold if precipitation starts to fall. And even if it's not pouring cats and dogs, if you chartered a guide and are on one of those glitzy, sparkle-plenty bass boats, you may need the rubberized yellow stuff anyway. When those motors kick into full throttle, "Bubba" may be heading you across the lake at 50 mph over to his favorite side of the pond. Friends, you will be sitting high up on a pedestal seat. Chances are good to excellent that there will not be any kind of windbreaker. A light chop on the lake will throw gallons of water over you and at that point, you may remember to thank me for this suggestion. Make absolutely certain that the foul weather gear has an attached hood to ensure full warmth.

Clothing For Much Saner Times

Forget the shorts, or bathing suits, no matter what! Yes, most fishermen you see in the summer are dressed in shorts, but for several reasons, that really makes no sense. Obviously, shorts often equate to a killer sunburn and no matter how you lather your body with sunscreen, its life expectancy may be surpassed by your time on the water. The resulting burn can ruin your whole day if not week. But also, the oil you use may get on your hands and then transferred to your hook or lure or bait, and the critters down below might not like its smell.

Yeah, we are trying to attract beginners and some of you may be on the water trying to attract another angler instead of a fish, so you may want to cuss me out now. Well, do your companion attracting another time and concentrate on impressing the person instead with the skill that you should acquire from reading this book!

Besides sunburn, every kind of flying wild life critter simply loves the appeal of skin. That translates into mosquitoes, bees, black flies, and the like. Nothing looks as silly as a pseudo angler does in skimpy attire swatting this way and that to defeat a winged invader.

White clothing works well when it's warm out, but make sure it's plenty cheap because a fish that tries to get rid of a deep-swallowed hook could mess your attire up permanently. (The fish will up-chuck much of its stomach contents onto your shirt and/or pants). I usually wear dark clothing but truthfully, lighter is better when it really is hot out.

And now for the last bit of advice. Top your attire off with a cap. The so-called "baseball cap" is all you need, if it's not so cold that you need something warmer. If your skin is particularly sensitive to sun, you may want the kind that has flaps or a longer brim. So here is another "Gone Fishin'" secret to share.

SHH: Tie it on! Nothing is as useless as a cap that flies off your head as the boat moves a bazillion miles an hour. They are easy to pick up if you are using an electric motor and it's broad daylight out, but what if you are standing on a pier and the wind lifts the doggone thing off and it winds up 50 feet away? I always tie one end of four feet of line to the band of the cap and the other end gets attached to a belt loop on my pants. I call that "Hat Insurance," and you cannot imagine how many times I've simply plucked the hat out of the air and plopped it back onto my head. And, yes, you are welcome!

Saltwater Clothing

Go back to the freshwater section and simply follow the instructions you find there. For nearly every instance on saltwater, your preparations for attire will match most of the things I want you to wear in freshwater. But since it is possible that you will be far, far away from land, if your saltwater outing is in the winter, it is even more important to stay warm at all times. Yes, the boat may have a heated cabin but if the fish are biting, you won't want to go inside. Therefore, stress warmth!

Make certain you wear a two-pocket shirt in cold weather and have the chemically treated warmers in each one.

And do you remember the "Hat Insurance" we discussed earlier? If your hat blows off way out to sea, it is long gone and forgotten so never venture out on deck without a length of line attaching the cap to your pants!

I know that you may have to be given a push to get your feet in motion because of all the clothing that I want you to wear, but salt or fresh, you may need it all!

CHAPTER 11

Freshwater Boats

Let's break this down into a few categories — bigger water vs. smaller water, and the difference between the two is key to what kind of boat you should fish from.

Small Water

Define small, someone once asked me. Well, small water is the kind that you can both see across and maybe even swim across — and no super star swimmers either, just the doggie paddle variety. "Small" applies to ponds and little streams or rivers, provided that the "moving" water is not fast.

And therefore, small water could also be called "safe water," in brief. In such water, any manner of leak-proof craft can be put in if you are alone or may have one other person to fish with. However, smaller boats often are quite tipsy too, so no matter how little a spot, do make certain that you and anyone with you can swim (in case you turn the boat over in excitement or clumsiness).

A little boat could be a canoe or "Johnboat," or any kind of rowboat, with or without an engine. Do make certain that if you launch a small vessel, you always have a flotation device with you for every boat occupant. In fact, it would behoove you to have everyone wear a Coast Guard approved life jacket, just in case.

I don't know who came up with the name "Johnboat," really. Probably a fellow named "John," I suppose. But a Johnboat is far from safe, especially the little 8-10 foot variety. And even the 12-16 footers may be unsafe for big water. The basic design of such a craft involves the front end being rather snub-nosed, cut sharply across its bow in fact. You see, as the boat moves forward, if enough wave action takes place and heavyweight Uncle Luke is sitting in the front seat, the front of the boat may actually dunk itself into the drink. Such a dunking can be both wet and dangerous. It is not uncommon for an inexperienced boater to overcompensate at such times and this is often when a boat rolls over. The bow can actually dip deeply into the water and draw many gallons into the boat. Panic is a dangerous element and when a wall of water invades the inside of your boat, fright often takes over.

Sure, the better "Johnboats" have adequate Styrofoam or other flotation equipment securely fastened under each seat as well as within its inner sides. And yes, because of that the boat may not actually sink. But they can and often do wallow in the water with virtually no forward movement. Even with an engine running, the boat cannot go anywhere. Hunters really love to seek their prey on the water via a Johnboat; however, 99% of the time they hug a shoreline and use the boat for transportation to a hidden away "blind," on shore. Their vessel is more like a short distance transporter instead of a serious boat for riding around in.

We have all seen and most of us have been in a canoe of one kind or another. Yes, they move fast if you know how to paddle, and are in fact, fun, but for fishing? Maybe not. I had a friend who loved his canoe and fished in it many days a year, but he was very smart. He rigged it with pontoons on each side that added an incredible amount of stability to the boat. It remained quite lightweight, but it was virtually unsinkable because of the two aluminum pontoons that held the boat afloat.

Big Water

The more traditional vessel found on most freshwater spots is either made out of aluminum or fiberglass. Fiberglass is heavier and as a result, far more stable a platform. Bigger water translates into larger, safer boats and if you are about to visit a large lake, make sure your boat is sturdy enough to handle the venue.

If you really get into fishing and like privacy, a small but safe boat may be what you want. You can buy a used boat but make certain that it is leak-proof and if you purchase it with an engine, have a mechanic with you to make sure the "kicker" does its putt-putt thing well. The last thing you want to do is buy a boat that has a hidden crack that was welded but might soon pop open. And even if the boat is dry and tight, if the engine doesn't work, woe is you out there a mile from shore when the wind starts to crank up. So buy used to save money, but make certain that an expert helps you determine its quality.

Most small boats that are used on bigger water are built for safety. They are vee-nosed and have sloped decks. Some come with a flat bottom but key here is not only the shape of the boat but its weight. The lightest boat imaginable may be very easy to launch but it also is easiest to tip!

Besides using your own boat, joining a club that has members who have their own rigs would be a fine way to start out. This way, your fellow club members just might share some of their vast knowledge with you.

As we will talk about later in connection with saltwater fishing, chartering your own boat is the best way, by far, to start out. Hey, if you are out on one of the Great Lakes and ten-foot waves knock you to your knees or worse, get you hanging over the rail, that's just your own tough luck if you are with a group. But if you chartered the boat yourself and you cannot handle the rough water, just tell the skipper to head back to the barn. Your captain depends on publicity and that is caused by a good catch so if you tie up without scoring, that is not good, but again, you paid the money so it's your call to return home. Presuming you have good weather, to get into more when we get to salt, a charter could be a wonderful way for you to learn many of the intricate details required for success.

SHH: Well, not at all a secret, but something you really need to know, is the need to have a sonar device on your boat, no matter how little the boat or small the body of water you fish — fresh, or saltwater. Some come permanently affixed to the bigger boats and others are quite portable. They serve a myriad of purposes, from determining water depth and slope, to reading schools of fish. Buy one!!

Engines

Again, let's not try to create an expert, just a fisherman. So we won't get into the technical stuff like "4-stroke" vs. diesel vs. long shaft, etc. Honestly, what you want is an engine that will start with the first or second pull of the rope or turn of the key. And you want one that will take you from here to there and back in the shortest period of time. And to do that, again, if you are not a mechanic yourself, I suggest you buy new. Alternatively, if you seek "used," as just noted, have a mechanic with you and make sure the seller allows you to try the motor out on a nearby lake.

Some waters have restricted use regulations. Many will not allow an engine to be used if they are in excess of, for example, 10 horsepower. So know where you will fish and what the rules are before you shop for a motor.

Electric motors are a wonderful means of transportation on smaller bodies of water. In fact, even on big lakes, coming and going can be done via a 150-h.p. kicker but trolling at slow speed is often best with an electric engine. Some guys like to rig the engine up in the stern and others up forward. If your boat is large enough and you have adequate mechanical skill, by all means, rig the engine up at the front end of the boat. Larger boats are steered with a steering wheel positioned mid-ships and the more traditional "bass boats" run from the front end. A foot-pedal arrangement is built in which actually allows an experienced angler to fish by hand and drive by foot all at the same time. When you have acquired enough skill to do this without having nearby boaters point and laugh at you, you have arrived!

Lots of the bigger bass boats have a monster sized gasoline engine (or two) in the rear with two electric kickers as well, one at each end of the boat. Call these guys anything but "Clem" or "J.R." and they may not be able to respond. By the way, a "bass-boat" comes with several key elements. In no particular order, they have:

- padded decks for quiet;

- enough rod holders to place thirty eleven rods in;

- storage space to hold nineteen tackle boxes filled with every plastic lure known to man;

- a large live bait well to hold your catch in so that they can later release them; and

- for certain, something big to store their beer in.

When you get beyond 18-20 feet of boat, you are either highly skilled already, or have enough money to hire a skipper, so we won't get into these boats because our target angler here is the beginner.

SHORE FISHING: This may be the best way for a beginner to start. Having no boat means less to think about. However, "shore-line" can be very tough to find other than for trout anglers. But nearly all lakes and ponds everywhere do offer at least some amount of legal access for shore fishermen.

Knowledge of casting is more important, unless you are fishing very close to the shore for smaller fish. Spinning gear is essential for long casts. The terminal tackle used from a boat will work well from land, of course. Instead of slider floats, one can generally have luck with typical bobbers instead.

What is helpful from shore is the use of a rod holder. Any manner of device will work, from the store-bought variety (metal pole that sticks into the ground which has an arm to rest the pole onto), to the knife-cut forked stick.

SHH: When using anything that props your rod up, make certain to have the fishing line sit on the other side of the "fork" as the rod rests within the fork. This way, if a big fish suddenly slams your bait, the line will not be stuck under the rod. Otherwise, the rod could be launched out like a harpoon. Needed too is the proper adjustment of your "drag" so that line can be pulled off the reel on a sudden and fierce bite.

SHH: When fishing in moving water from the bank, you can either hold to bottom with heavy weight or bounce downstream. If bouncing is your goal, with lure or bait, note this carefully, please. Most of your bites will occur as the bait or lure starts to lift off bottom on its downstream roll. Look at your watch with me — if the line is going from left to right, your bites will occur more often at 1:30 as the lift begins. Fishing current from right to left, the best hits will usually occur at 10:30.

CHAPTER 12

Saltwater Fishing

"Charter" Boats

A "charter" boat is one that has a captain who is licensed to take anglers out for a day or partial day of fishing. Generally, the Coast Guard requires such a skipper to hold a license, which requires far more skill than the weekend fisherman has. Tests have to be passed, and not just regarding boat-handling skills. Drug tests also are involved, to make sure that the passengers are protected. Perhaps the best way to start you out as a beginner, if you can afford it, is to charter a boat. Do it with a group of friends or relatives, of if you have the money to spare, hire the boat for your own use. This way, the captain and mate will be your personal "crew" and a world of teaching will be yours for the asking. Begin with a half-day of fishing, in a time of the year when weather should be good. If the offshore forecast is for tolerable weather you will be required to go, or lose your money. But if it is really stinko out, the captain will either refund your deposit or reschedule for another day.

Again, a half-day should be your start, and not at night either. It could get too cold for you, and it is more difficult to learn in the dark. Try for protected waters as well, to give you the top chance at comfort for trip #1.

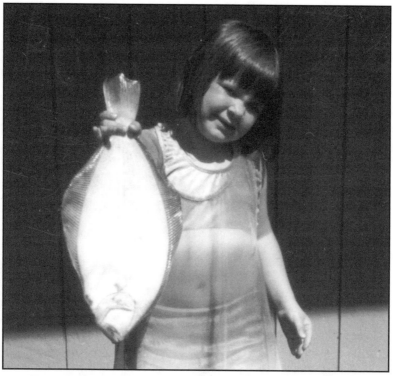

*Three-year old Nicole Hauburger caught this 18-inch fluke
on board her Aunt Judie's boat, the "Hey Jude,"
in the calm waters of Shinnecock Bay, New York.*

"Open And Head" Boats

Head or open or party or drift boats are all a variation of one and the same thing. "Open or head" means that they take fishermen out one head at a time, and are "open" to the public, not privately chartered to a group. I never could figure out why they are called "party" boats in the northeastern part of America, but they are. They really do not allow "parties" at all and many restrict the volume of alcoholic beverages an angler may bring on board and/or consume. For sure, fishermen cannot "party" with drugs because the Coast Guard can arrest such a user (and even is allowed to confiscate the boat from its owner!) And some are called "drift boats," especially in and around Florida, because these vessels get

Sue Wohlford of Puyallup, Washington fished with Denny's Guide Service of Sitka, Alaska and caught this 50-pound chinook salmon. (And how easy was it for her to stand up?)

to a fishing spot, stop, and drift as you fish for critters down below. Boats "drift fish" everywhere, but for some reason, they are not normally called "drift boats" other than near Florida.

Such vessels go out for four, six, and eight hours. The more exotic ones leave ports in California, Florida, Rhode Island, Massachusetts, and elsewhere and don't get back to the barn for many an hour. Some of the California vessels stay out for a week or two at a time. Of course if you are a beginner, this style of fishing can be a sink or swim adventure for you, but it really is as dumb a thing as you can do. Forgetting the fact that bigger fish are involved than a starter may be able to handle, bigger waves too are a basic rule of thumb. If you are out there on the 20th hour of a 48-hour trip and your belly button is hanging out of your mouth for the past hour, don't you really know right then that you did a dopey thing? Never, not ever, should a beginner do more than a four or maybe six-hour trip on day one, regardless of how you handle waves on your frou-frou sailboat. The smell of diesel, combined with the stink of bait and mess caused by fish slopping all over the deck could be just what the doctor ordered to get you into the worst kind of seasickness imaginable.

So if you are like most people and money is important, board a headboat that fishes close to the dock for 4-6 hours and try for a weekday if you can. This is so that you can be on a less crowded boat, which allows you to pick the brain of the mate(s) for assistance. Assistance in handling the gear, baiting up, and removing fish from the hooks, and so on.

SHH: Tipping the mate even before the boat sails is a good idea. Tell him that you are a beginner and will need help. And if you like the help you got, add another gratuity as you leave the boat at the end of the outing. If you did catch fish, and rules permit you to keep them, again tip the guy who cleans them for you and puts the fillets in a nice plastic bag.

DRIFTING: As just discussed in brief, a boat will often drift with the current in waters that generally are known to hold fish. The skipper may see the fish on his sonar, or may just (by instinct or prior knowledge) assume that fish should be near where he has the boat drifting. If you are in deep water and/or are after large fish, the side of the boat that gets the wind is the one that you want to be on, or you may even be required to fish from.

With wind blowing into your face, the boat is drifting away from the wind and your line will be positioned away from the boat. If you are on the other side of the boat your line will eventually swing under the boat and may even come up near the guys on the "better" side and tangle with them. So if you can, without being annoying, and presuming that space permits, always try to fish on a drift from the side that gets your lines out and away. The first rod way up in the bow is a fine spot, but while you have a better chance at avoiding tangles here, you also will get bounced around more so if you fear mal de mer, the best end of the boat is its widest, the stern!

The more skillful skippers practice "Power drifting." Two engines are needed for this and if the guy knows what he is doing, your catch can improve. You see, if a boat is drifting, and the wind and tide stop, that ends the "drift." While many fish are caught at anchor, this usually relates to structure fishing, where the boat is positioned right over the top of a wreck or pile of rocks. Drifting, on the other hand, usually involves covering lots of open water with sand or maybe mud bottom. And if you aren't drifting, you are not covering territory and the fishing may slow down.

At such times your skipper will maneuver the boat sideways, kind of like that car that was built in the 70's. Using one engine and then the other, maybe one in reverse and the other slowly into forward position, an expert can actually create an artificial "drift," moving the boat sufficiently so that territory is covered.

THE ANGLE: Fish usually stay in place, face-into current or tide, whether treading water with their side fins, or holding down near bottom, nearly always. Sure, they will swim this way and that after bait, but when waiting to pounce, they stick headfirst into what is coming at them. They do this because it is more comfortable to them. And they do it too because baitfish, shrimp, crabs, and the like, will pass by in the current from up tide on down, and if they are looking ahead, the fish will get first grabs at the chow.

ANCHORED: While your boat is anchored, it often is best to fish in the very back of the boat because of the same reasons just discussed. The fish will hit bait that is going towards them. Critters behind the boat will inhale baits that slide downtide into their paths. Captain Pete Del Rossi of Fortescue, New Jersey taught me this years ago, and let me share what he suggested to me ... it is worth repeating.

SHH: We were anchored and fishing for sea trout (a/k/a weak-fish), and the tide had begun to get fast. Instead of using a heavier sinker in the back of the boat, he told me to put a smaller one on! I couldn't hold my bait at bottom near the stern this way so I asked him why. He showed me how to drop down with a little sinker and leave the reel open. As current took the sinker off bottom, the line would release from the open spool and slide back across the bottom, heading down current. This kept my bait bouncing on bottom all the time and reached out to fish that were well behind the boat. I caught 41 weakfish that day, far more than are now legally permitted, and my three companions who wouldn't take Pete's advice had less than that total between them!

CHUMMING: Fishing downtide is even more important when chumming. While chum is being ladled out for bluefish, tuna, etc, allowing your baited hook to slide out downtide and follow the chum "slick" will double or triple your catch.

ROTATE FISH: I fished a charter boat out of Green Harbor, Massachusetts once and the skipper actually required us to rotate fish. What does "rotate fish" mean? The angler who was in the corner of the boat that faced straight out best was usually the one who caught a fish. He then had to move to the worst angle out. Usually, it was the guy in the corner whose big chrome jig was taken before the other three of us. So we had to actually rotate to give each of us the best position for our jig to face the waiting fish.

Fishing From Land And Piers

In a calm saltwater spot, angle is not very important. But when the water is moving, you need both a proper angle to position you correctly so that a fish can find your offering, as well as enough weight. Lures must be of sufficient weight to get you out there and still drop deep enough to reach the fish. And the same thing applies in connection with bait — your sinker has to hold bottom, unless you are intentionally bottom bouncing.

Casting and retrieving bait will work best with either a flat or an egg sinker. These will permit you to move bait back to where you are standing with the least amount of hanging in bottom permissible. On the other hand, if you want to stay put, especially in the surf, pyramid shaped sinkers are really essential.

Most fish will face into the tide. If you are using two hooks on your line from shore, even if the fish are really "bottom fish," try this —

SHH — Instead of rigging so that both hooks drop below your sinker, tie one so that it rides above the sinker and the other below. The top hook should be on a short leader, not more than six inches, tied in, maybe 18 inches above the sinker. While just letting the outfit sit in a rod holder, the top hook will generally get at least twice as many bites as the bottom one. The top hook will drift around in tide, dusting bottom, and the low hook will not move much at all.

CHAPTER 13

Terminal Tackle
(Fresh & Saltwater)

LURES: Assorted devices, called "lures," are made to look like native food for the fish. Whether you are fishing in salt or freshwater, a wide variety of lures are on the market and more are being made every day. Let's break them into a few basic groupings —

"Stickbaits"

Salt or fresh, big or small, these are lures (commonly called "plugs") that are made to attract fish to them. Some have built in rattles to appeal to the hearing of the fish. Many are one piece and some come jointed to wiggle more in the water. Most of them used to be hand carved out of wood but now 99%+ are created out of plastic. As many colors as you can imagine are put into plugs, but the basic concept usually involves trying to match the color of the baitfish that are in the water that you are fishing in. Yes, we have all seen bright yellow, maybe chartreuse, or such colors on plugs and they

Stickbait.

even catch fish. But for the most part, the stickbait should look like food not freak to Ms. Fish!

"Jerkbaits" are similar to stickbaits by the way, but require different movement to attract fish. Stickbaits will produce well for trollers or guys casting and retrieving in a variety of ways. But "jerkbaits" should be jerked during their retrieve for top results.

Such plugs are made to either float or sink. If you are after deep-water fish, a diving or sinking plug may do best. Some that sink do so ever so slowly and even have instructions that teach you how to "count down" as in "one-one thousand, two-one thousand, etc, as the plug heads to the bottom. The box may say that you should turn the handle and close the reel at a count of, say four, to be in the best comfort zone of your walleye, bass, etc.

Soft Lures

Plastic usually, but most guys call them "rubber" as a habit. Many are mounted on a large hook with a small weight behind the hook's eye to allow the lure to sink. Most of the hooks are made to be "weed-less," to keep them from getting hung in bottom. Soft baits of every kind, color and size are on the market and they do work. Many of the manufacturers have put arti-ficial smells right within the material of these lures to further appeal to the fish.

A soft lure.

Metal Lures

"Block tin squids" were, once upon a time, the most popular in the northeast for saltwater guys. World War II survival kits actually held some of these, in case a sailor was shipwrecked. They saved many lives by producing catches of fish on the dacron lines that were also placed in the kits. But nowadays, a metal lure is made to flash and shine as it is either jigged or trolled in the water, and this applies in both fresh and salt. Arguably, half or more of the salmon that are trolled all over America, from Alaska to the Great

Lakes and beyond, are caught on little skinny metal "spoons" that come in a variety of metal finishes and painted colors.

Metal lures are made to be completely metal or not. Besides the one-piece jigs, many are made with plastic or hair attachments and these are generally used in sweetwater. Among the names for such lures are "Pig'n jig." They come with metal and plastic or hair and the hook often is adorned with a strip of pre-cut pork rind, thus the name "PIG" of the pig 'n jig, got it? Other lures that are - commonly used, generally in sweetwater by bass and pike anglers, are called spinner or buzz baits. Most of them are made in a "weed-less" manner so that they can be cast into and pulled through weeds where big fish hide.

"In-line" spinners are very popular members of the metal clan. A skinny metal loop is attached onto your line or swivel, and its business end usually has a treble hook. Between the attachment loop and hooks is a swinging blade that flutters wildly as the lure is retrieved. This is called an "in-line" spinner.

Flies
'Nuff said. Be you Zane Gray or a rank amateur, the number of flies that are made to fool anything from little trout to monster sailfish is unlimited. As noted earlier, a gang of books have been written just about fly fishing so if that is what you want to do, finish reading this book and then buy a couple of fly fishing books.

Floats
BOBBERS: You can usually tell who a beginner is by the size of the float that he puts on his line. If the bobber goes kabloom when it hits the water, that fellow just began. The biggest, dopiest floats on earth are those that starter uppers purchase. If it looks like a two-tone tennis ball, they buy it. However, unless you are after gigantic fish, don't even think of buying something so large.

The traditional float comes in red and white or maybe yellow and orange, and is far smaller than a ping-pong ball (maybe half that size in fact), so use that as a basic rule of thumb. They come with a clip at both ends. Just determine how deep you want your bait to

Here's the float!

Use a small float like this youngster on the right is using at the Newtown Township, Pennsylvania fishing class run by Fish 'N Tales. (A different net wouldn't hurt though.)

dangle in the water and clip your line at the top of the float at that distance from where your hook will be. If the float still slides down because the clip isn't tight enough, then fasten the bottom clip of the float below the top, and that should get your bobber positioned just right.

Some floats come with glow in the dark tape and others have pointy ends that stick up. But the old round bobber is really the best. You may want one in cork but again, the circle is easiest to use.

The main reason to vary from a traditional bobber is if you want to fish with a float but still get down deep. For example, with a seven-foot rod you can rig a bobber at four feet with ease, and still be able to cast out. If you use a short rod with large drop, chances are good to excellent that you will not be able to swing out and get any distance at all. Worse, you might hook yourself or a nearby companion. And then came the "slider float."

"Slider" Floats

A "slider float" (a/k/a "slip-bobber") is a wonderful tool which permits an angler to set their float at a pre-determined depth so that they can fish deep and still be able to cast far away from the boat. I have actually fished with a slider float that allowed me to fish 50 feet down. Rather than try to explain the method of rigging it, I suggest you go to your favorite tackle dealer and ask to see a few samples. Most of them are three inches long and are capable of supporting a ¼ ounce sinker and a good-sized live baitfish. The better ones have instructions printed right on the package. They work, great!

So, want to look like you never fished before? Take a surf rod to your local lake and attach a big enough bobber that can keep a brick afloat, and maybe wear white clothing so that you can get nasty, dirty fish yuck embedded thereon.

Sinkers

We've got bank, pyramid, flat, round, bell, egg, split-shot, and lots more to pick from and each has its own proper use.

BANK SINKERS: Starting off with bank, the most commonly used sinker, this is shaped a little like a pear with a hole on the skinny, top end, to tie your line onto. Normally used in saltwater, some anglers who fish from shore like to use these same sinkers from land.

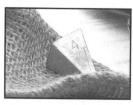

PYRAMID SINKERS: A pyramid sinker is shaped like an upside down pyramid, with a metal loop embedded into the top to tie onto. The pyramid is hardly ever used other than as a means of holding onto bottom when current or waves are smashing. So, for example, go with one from the surf. Maybe you could need one in strong current in freshwater too, but that would be a very rare occurrence.

4 oz. pyramid sinker.

FLAT SINKERS: Guys who like to cast often use flat sinkers. They need the weight to get out, but don't want to get hung in bottom so they cast and start a very slow retrieve of their baited

*Here's
the ba
sinker*

*Ron Jacobsen took this photo of three smiling kids at Cedar Brook
Park Pond, Plainfield, New Jersey. Note the bank sinker
being used for this fine channel catfish.*

hooks as soon as they reach bottom. Soft bottom like sand or mud
is where they get the greatest use. The sinker holds you down at
bottom as you pull your hooks back to you, past the waiting fish.

ROUND SINKERS: Rounded sinkers are coming on strong and
I have found that lots of small boat anglers really like them. They
don't get hung up often, and still can be cast and retrieved. Just
remember to not use one any heavier than is needed.

BELL SINKERS: A bell-shaped sinker is just that, with a place
on top to tie onto. Many of us old-timers still call them "dipsey"
sinkers and I have no clue why! They hold bottom well in most
instances because the heaviest part of them is at their lower end.
Lots of sweetwater anglers like to use these from shore to get a
good hold in place.

EGG SINKERS: Egg sinkers are made to look like an egg with
two open ends. Fishermen put their line through one end and out
the other. Not made to hold bottom at all, instead, the egg will slide

along in current or wind but still try to keep you down near bottom, or maybe suspended, where you feel the fish are residing. In my own personal experience, I use these more than any other sinker out there now. Whether you are fishing bottom for lake trout, or maybe hanging suspended for hybrid bass, as well as bouncing along in a drift while angling for mutton snapper, they work each time.

PINCH-ON SINKERS: Pinch-on (split-shot) sinkers come in a variety of sizes with them as small as the name we used to use, "bee-bee's," up to a half or even a full-ounce. Most of the time, they are put into play in sweetwater to get baits down a bit in the water column. But I've seen them used in salt as well to allow a chunk of butterfish to reach down to where the marauding schools of bluefish are ready to chomp. A variety is called (and may even wear a patented name) "rubber-core." They have ends that pinch onto your line, but each end is protected from cutting your line by the insertion of a bit of rubber as a buffer. Nice idea!

Swivels

The main use for a swivel is to allow you to fish in a variety of ways without getting your fishing line tangled badly. If you tie your line directly to your lure and cast and retrieve often enough, trouble may lie ahead. And if you hook a few big critters and try to reel back in quickly, without a swivel you surely will develop twists in your line that could cause problems later on. Again, a wide variety is on the market. Let's discuss some now —

SNAP-SWIVELS: Snap-swivels may be the ones most purchased, for fresh as well as saltwater. Simple enough: tie your line onto the circular top of the swivel and open the other end, called "snap." Attach the lure of your choice to the snap end and close it tightly to keep the lure fastened tight.

THREE-WAY SWIVELS: Three-way swivels are very popular, mostly in salt. They have three metal loops. Tie your line onto one end. Now tie a short leader onto another, and put your sinker on the end of that leader to hold bottom. Depending on what you are fishing for, your hook goes on the other loop. A "snelled" (see

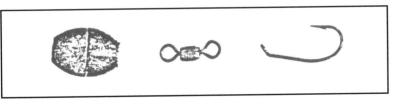

*¾ oz. egg sinker, black barrel swivel, and #6 Sproat hook,
in the right order for proper rigging!*

hooks soon) hook is last but not least. You may put a six-inch one
on, all the way up to a six footer.

BARREL-SWIVELS: Barrel swivels are put into place nearly
every time you use an egg sinker. Slip your line through an egg
sinker and tie that end fast to the top of your barrel swivel. Use a
barrel as small as you need, but be careful that it isn't so little that
your swivel can get caught up into the opening of your egg sinker.
And now tie on a leader from the bottom of the barrel down to your
hook.

FISH-FINDER RIGS: These are a combination of things, really.
It is a complicated version of a swivel, but one that adds significant
numbers to your scorecard at times. Use of a fish-finder involves a
combination of plastic and metal, usually with your line, leadered
hook, swivel and sinker all being melded perfectly together into
use.

When rigged right, your sinker will stay at bottom while the
leadered hook can be dragged away by a fish who has no clue that
someone is up there trying to hurt them. Generally used on boats,
I have done exceedingly well from shore while fishing for striped
bass with them. You can also do this from land when freshwater
fishing.

Leaders

Leaders come in the same diameter as the line on your reel, up
to ten times that, and in mono, fluorocarbon, or maybe wire,
depending on the what and where. The key is try to avoid use of a
leader that holds your hook on with lighter line than that which you
have on your reel. I have found that the leader tangles terribly

around the line if it is skinnier than the reel's line.

Fluorocarbon leaders are used below a barrel swivel to keep a wary fish from being scared away. Anglers feel that such nearly invisible leader adds greatly to their score.

Wire leaders are put into play when after critters that have serious choppers. In freshwater, pike, muskies, etc., are those that can cut your regular leader in a heartbeat. Out in the briny, the numbers are far greater. Most commonly, barracuda, king mackerel and bluefish top the list of fish that will clip you off in an instant. There exists a school of thought that says that while you may get cut off without metal, you might get two or three times as many bites without it too. You see, some fish will recognize the wire as something that presents bait or lure in a non-lifelike manner and avoid it. Again, speaking from personal experience, I get five times as many bites from pike without wire, and may get chopped a few times, but don't have any concern about it because I know that I will have more action sans metal.

Hooks

Here's a simple formula to follow. No /0 means smaller and any /0 number means bigger, got it? And now to explain further. If you buy a size 10 hook it is very small indeed, maybe meant for sunfish or small flounder. But if you tie a size 10/0 hook on, you have a piece of steel that can hold bottom by itself. It is intended for the largest of fish because it has a huge gap opening.

Hooks come in "circle" style. They are shaped like a semi-circle and regular anglers feel they produce the biggest bite to catch ratio. These same fishermen feel that they don't even have to reach back to the sky while setting a rod to a bite when they have a "circle" on.

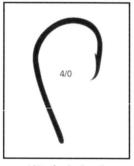

4/0 circle hook.

Traditional hooks really have two other basic shapes. They are offset or non-offset. Yes, some have pointy top ends and others are rounded. Others have a very wide-gap but back to the basics, we have "offset" or "non-offset."

An offset hook is one that has its barb pointed away from the top bend of the hook. A non-offset one has the barb right in line with the top. For the most part, I like to use non-offset hooks with live bait and offset ones otherwise. If clam, dead shrimp, or worms are the bait, I normally use an offset one, also called "beak," like the beak of an eagle.

My own experience with live bait has me using the non-offset ones because I often miss fish on setting with live bait if I have an offset hook tied on. (The hook often gets doubled around backwards and stuck a second time into the body of my baitfish with an offset hook.)

Let your mate tell you what size hook to use, or at least talk to a knowledgeable tackle store dealer when you say where you intend to go fishing. For heavens sake, don't buy size 10/0's when fishing for little critters, or vice-versa, the guys will giggle at you, and maybe call you what you are here to avoid hearing, "beginner!"

Some hooks are mounted on their own leaders ("snelled") and others are tied directly to your line. In sweetwater, as often as possible, avoid the leadered hooks and instead tie it fast onto your line. Again, a fellow club member or mate should be consulted with.

Knots

Are you a Boy Scout, or maybe a Boatswain's Mate in the Navy? If not, forget about multiple knots, please. Yes, you will get better breaking strength with a double-bend hammer nail over and under knot, but you may also spend far too much time in the process. And worse yet, the more complicated the knot, the better your chance at creating a "curly-queue."

Never create a curly queue? Oh yeah, you are a beginner. Every angler on earth has done so, and the only good part of this takes place if no one is with you. You see, a curly queue is created as a badly tied knot opens up and your line comes free from your hook. The end of the line looks all twisted, like curly queue pasta.

And now for the worst part. This usually takes place when you lose a fish. We all have been known to lie, saying that we lost the fish to a weak spot. Never that we broke the line because we applied too much pressure in fighting the fish. And for sure, never, not ever, that we tied the knot badly. Well, go with a simple but good knot most of the time and you will nearly always avoid this.

Yes, if you are tying fly line to mono, it's more complicated. And if you want to attach mono to the skinny synthetics, worse yet. But line to a hook, swivel, sinker or lure? Hell, a three to five turn clinch knot is all you should need. Better yet would be the use of an "improved clinch knot," but more care is needed to get this one tight enough to avoid a "curly queue."

When tying line to line, a double clinch or "barrel" (also known as "blood") knot is tied and, you will learn how to do both of these after two or three tries.

Here's How To Tie An Improved Clinch Knot

IMPROVED CLINCH KNOT

1. An old standby. Pass line through eye of hook, swivel or lure. Double back and make five turns around the standing line. Hold coils in place; thread end of line through first loop above the eye, then through big loop, as shown.

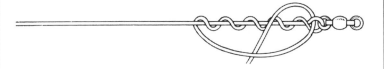

2. Hold tag end and standing line while coils are pulled up. Take care that coils are in spiral, not lapping over each other. Slide tight against eye. Clip tag end.

Here's How To Tie
A Simplified Barrel Or Blood Knot

SIMPLIFIED BLOOD KNOT

1. Take the two lines' ends
   and tie a simple over-
   hand knot (which will be
   clipped off later). Then
   tighten to combine the
   two lines into one.

2. Form a loop where the two lines meet, with the overhand knot in
   the loop. Pull one side of the loop down and begin taking turns
   with it around the standing line. Keep point where turns are made
   open so turns gather equally on each side.

3. After eight to ten turns, reach through center opening and pull
   remaining loop (and overhand knot) through. Keep finger in this
   loop so it will not spring back.

   Hold loop with teeth and pull both ends of line, making turns
   gather on either side of loop.

4. Set knot by pulling lines as tightly as possible. Tightening coils
   will make loop stand out perpendicular to line. Then clip off the
   loop and overhand knot close to the newly formed knot.

CHAPTER **14**

Fish Cleaning

L et's not make this about what kind of fish are healthy and which are not, okay? Clearly, there are some fish that are caught somewhere that are not especially good to eat. Some carry mercury or PCB and others have acid rain problems. And yes, other material which can hurt. But what about pigs? And maybe, what about chickens? And, oh yeah, even though the FDA may inspect beef, pork, and the like, did they really examine your own personal steak, or do they check out random selections? Do you really think that each and every machine gets a personal inspection?

So do take health department advisories seriously, but unless the fish comes out of really bad water, or a specific advisory has been published about a certain species out of a body of water, don't get nuts. Most advisories deal with prospective problems that could hurt small children or women who are or want to get pregnant. My dad died as a result of an environmental problem (he smoked and worked with asbestos) so I do not take health advisories lightly, but I don't dwell on them to a fault!

The best way by far to prepare your catch for the table is to pay someone to do it! If you are involved with a charter or open boat, the mate or maybe even the skipper of a small boat will be glad to

Captain Bob Murphy guided Tonya Harpold to her first hybrid bass ever at Lake Conroe, Texas. Bob often fillets fish with an electric knife — and no, I am not nor ever will I be that good!

clean your catch. A "tip" is mandatory but at times, I have seen certain very specific rates charged for cleaning. Back in the 70's when the flounder run was on in significant numbers there were always a half-dozen guys around the dock at Quincy, Massachusettes who would fillet your fish for as little as nickel or a dime per fish. And when codfish literally paved the bottom off of George's Bank, a quarter per baccala was the rate.

SHH: But if you want to clean fish yourself, here's one very key thing to learn. As in humans, fish have a gall bladder. If you accidentally pierce the gall with your knife, it will spill yellowish liquid out into the closest flesh of the fish. This certainly will not kill you, but wow, it surely will make that part of the fish taste terribly bitter. So by all means, watch out for this, because your kid or better half may get stuck eating a forkful of yuck and you may permanently lose the best excuse you have for fishing, "They make good food and save us money, honey!" (RIGHT.)

Learn how to clean your catch by watching the mate. Just ask him to move slower and tip bigger. You hardly ever will need to remove the scales of the fish unless you want to eat the fish off of its framework. So filleting is what you want to learn.

Flatfish like flounder may be easiest, but some flatfish have their stomachs on one side of their body and some on the other. I won't bore you with which is which. Simply enough, feel the critter. If the white side is soft on one section, that is where the stomach is. Avoid this, because if you stick the knife in here you could hit that devil gall bladder.

Most flatfish are best cleaned by running a sharp and skinny knife down the white side from head to tail. You will follow the lateral line of the fish and if cut well, you can then slide the knife from this center bone down to the fins and produce a nice fillet. This fillet will be easy to remove the skin from, after you mess up the first two or three fish. Just put the fillet down on a board, skin side down, and slide the flat knife between skin and flesh and follow it until you have peeled off all the skin. Messy at first, after a while you will be able to produce a very nice hunk of boneless white meat. I suggest you first do the belly side and then the back

Michael Penkowen (age 7) beat this 9-pound, 7-ounce fluke
near the Marine Park Bridge at Jamaica Bay, New York.
Note the stomach is on the right side of the white meat.
Cut around it to avoid the gall.

because the stomach meat is thinner and more difficult to get done as a result.

More conventional fish like trout, bass, and mackerel, are generally easy to fillet after you get used to it. Always start up behind the head. Cut a thin ring around the fish from head to tail, not on its underside. Then work the knife down to the center bone, between flesh and bone, to its mid-way point (the center bone), and then be very careful. It's easy to slide the knife down the back end to the bottom fins and cut away your fillet. It's tougher to do this up near the head because you will wind up in the mushy stuff. Be super careful here because of the devil gall.

Clearly, if you are after a cleaned fish that isn't filleted, they are easier to do. But we now get back to your kid and/or better half and if they gag on a bone, there goes your excuse, again!

To clean a fish the old way, buy a scaler and scrape off all the scales. Then use your sharp knife to cut through the back right behind the head down to and through the center bone. Stop before you hit the gall, and cut on a slant backwards until you are parallel to the fish's refuse dump site. Yes, you may want to cut from its solid waste opening back up to the underside of the head to remove all of its entrails first but that is not really necessary.

Under few if any circumstances should you come home and throw the fish into the sink and say something like "Okay honey, I caught 'em, you clean 'em!" For sure, don't follow it up with "get me a beer, willya?" That hardly ever works any longer, and in fact hardly ever worked ever! You may never be able to go fishing again!

Under just about every circumstance you will encounter is the extreme need to keep your fish cold, whole, or filleted. Their flesh breaks down and the fish actually begins to go bad if kept in the open sun or in a bag or cooler that doesn't have ice in it. So by all means, on land or in a boat, do try to have your own sufficiently large cooler with ice in it. Put your freshly caught fish inside and if possible, have the mate put your filleted fish into plastic baggies and then into the cooler. Your fish will certainly taste much better and the chance of them spoiling will be next to zero this way.

CHAPTER 15

Cooking Fish

"**S**ushi" is, to me, BAIT, not food for the table. Whether you are out there on the west coast or maybe even farther, like say in Japan, or on the other hand, anywhere else, you may argue with me. But I just cannot get past the fact that that stuff is RAW, and raw fish means bait to me, not food for me, okay? So eat all the raw fish you want, go for it, I will not argue with you because it just might be that tuna, salmon, etc., tastes better uncooked. Good — but not for me, please. So let's cook some up now.

Fried Fish

Far and away the most popular method of cooking fish in all of America, and maybe elsewhere, is fried fish. In the United Kingdom, "fish & chips" rules. Every fast food restaurant from one end of the universe to the other serves fried fish. It could be "mystery meat" (unknown fish that is ground up and formed into a "fillet," like some do with chicken.) But more often than not, fried fish in most restaurants are true fillets that are cut out of a fresh fish into meal-size portions, breaded, and then flash frozen.

Perhaps the simplest method of frying fish involves a very large and deep frying pan or basket with clean oil. Get your fillets lined

The Tonking family ate like the dickens for several days with this great fighting and super tasting mess of hybrid bass they caught with Captain Bob Murphy at Lake Conroe, Texas.
Bake, broil or fry 'em.

up first. You may want to rinse them off and pat them dry, just in case there's any unwanted residue.

Have several things at the ready. Start off with a soup dish with a few well-beaten eggs. For sure, another dish with plain or seasoned breadcrumbs, depending on your own personal taste. Some folks like to also dip the fillets into a dish of white wine and/or lemon juice.

Dunk the fish into the wet stuff first, and then into the eggs, and lastly, into the breadcrumbs. Make certain to get the whole piece of fish well slathered in any of the substances you use to ensure the ultimate in taste.

Not really "heart-healthy," but if you aren't concerned about such things, next comes that frying container. (See "Sautéed fish" for heart-healthy.) Get the oil well heated before carefully (don't get splatter on you) placing the fillets in. Test it for heat first by putting a drop or two of water in. If it snarls and grumbles, it is far too hot. But if it sizzles a little, it's ready.

This style works best by far with a deep pan. Just remember to have some paper towels next to the stove because when you are done cooking, you should lightly tap both sides of the cooked fish to remove excess oil.

Have two spatulas at the ready. You will have to do this if you aren't really "deep frying." Turning a piece of fish can be pure misery if it breaks. Using two flippers at the same time should keep this from taking place.

Control the heat on the stove. Not too hot, but for sure, not too little either because you want to cook the fish through and through. Yes, fancy restaurants cook fish and peddle it to you as "simmered." To me, that means half-raw. If the flesh glistens when you cut it with the fork, that may not be adequately cooked for you.

When the breading turns nice and brown, turn it over if you were not using a real deep pan. If the whole fillet is enveloped in oil, you will not need to turn it, of course. Do it again a few times. You can tell that your fish is cooked well but not burned when the breading separates just ever so little and some flesh can be seen splitting.

Friend, that is done to me. Eat it less cooked if you wish though, as many people prefer it that way. Trial and error alone will tell you what is right for you. If your pan is big enough you should be able to cook a mess of fish for your family quickly. Otherwise get ready to eat last and cook your own pieces after serving everyone else.

SHH: And now, the secret for the cook. Save the tail section of the fish or the underside of a flatfish for yourself. Those parts taste better — — — shh, don't tell!

Sautéed Fish

Kind of like frying, but far healthier by lots. We who have to be careful because of heart problems or other miseries might want to sauté instead. Go with that same frying pan, but instead of any old oil and deep frying, use extra virgin olive oil or whatever your doctor suggests instead. Don't fill the pan but instead just lightly cover it so that each piece of fish gets touched by the cooking oil.

Use egg whites or maybe "egg beater" or a variation of same instead of regular eggs to avoid the yolks. I dip my fillets into lemon juice and then into the egg mix and lastly into plain bread-crumbs. Next comes the rest of the deal as above, but rather than drowning the meat in bubbling oil, a light layer of olive or walnut oil works best for me.

In The Oven

Broiled or baked, it's up to you. What is needed is a real hot stove though, especially if you are broiling because the fish will dry in the process otherwise. Butter lovers will still dunk the meat in lemon or wine, but then they put the fillet on a cooking surface, and add melted butter (be quiet, my still slightly clogged artery) across the top of the meat. Honestly, cooked sufficiently, this really tastes great. You may want to add some paprika on top of the butter for color. A shpritz or two of parsley ain't bad either.

"Whole" And On The Bone

Last but not least is the way that so-called "real fish lovers" do it. They scale the whole fish, and remove fins, head and guts. The otherwise entire fish is placed into whatever of the above methods works for you best, and gets cooked. More time is needed because you have a thicker slab of meat — two sides and bones instead of a single-sided fillet. My dad swore that he loved fish this way better than any other method. When you cook "whole fish," be prepared for a talk-free meal. If speech is encouraged, gagging on bones could easily mess up the meal, big time.

CHAPTER 16

The License

L et's try to avoid the subject of right or wrong now, please. Most serious anglers have their own opinion regarding whether we should be required to have a license to fish or not. A driver's license demands knowledge and skill before you are allowed behind the wheel. But a fishing license (and, in fact, motor boat operators licenses too), simply asks you to cough up some money. Just about everyone I know feels that a license is very appropriate for freshwater, and most say "no way" to saltwater licenses, but again, let's leave the lectures to the politicians and the clubs to fight about.

In freshwater, even most civil libertarians will agree that it's okay because the state spends most of if not all of the fees to grow and stock all kinds of fish, as well as to enforce regulations on the books.

What you do need to know as a beginner though is that you may need to hold a license to enable you to go fishing. And don't try to "share" one either, because that is blatantly illegal just about everywhere. If there are two anglers who need to be licensed, you cannot get away with saying that all the rods were yours and "he was just holding one for me while I was taking care of a bladder need." Not gonna' happen, friend!

This book is intended for the use of all beginners, but in the case of two of our primary sources of readership, kids and senior citizens, many of them will not be required to hold a license. Be very careful with this subject, because laws differ from area to area. Generally speaking though, seniors either pay less for a license or don't even need one at all. And the same thing applies to many kids. The law says that kids can drive a car at a variety of ages depending on where they live. The same thing applies to a fishing license, but most areas demand a license for anyone who has reached their 16th birthday.

In saltwater, some places only require visitors to hold a license when fishing inshore, and others issue a license to the captain of the boat which permits all anglers on board to fish. Hey, before you go fishing, ask the tackle store salesperson who you bought your gear from if you must be licensed. Chances are good that they can sell you such a license too. And please, don't complain about its cost; most of these stores only make a half-dollar for every license they sell — and they are required to pay for and carry a bond that guarantees that they won't steal the government's money!

CHAPTER 17

"Catch And Release"

I have participated in and even organized several organizations that some felt were way over the top to an extreme. So when I discuss "P.E.T.A." with friends, I am always careful to note that they do have a point. However, that "point" is so far an extreme to me that I don't hesitate to say that I disagree with them.

And what is "P.E.T.A." all about? You all know about the people who are anti-fur, right? "People for the Ethical Treatment of Animals" is what P.E.T.A.'s acronym represents, and fur is merely one of their issues. When it comes to "catch and release," the more extreme believers in P.E.T.A. come across my bow and here is one of the areas that I disagree with them in.

The extremists argue that catching a fish and releasing it is a form of torture! They say that it is better to catch and keep a fish (maybe killing it quickly, I never did hear how they want to do this — gas, a needle, bullet to the brain, who knows?) than to release it. They (again, not all members, only those who are really way over the top), feel that fighting a fish to submission is cruel and unusual punishment and that once returned to the water, has been terribly stressed. Honestly, I don't know if they recommend fish psychiatrists or not, but maybe so.

*Six-year old Hanks Flanagan of New Jersey put this
7-pound, 3-ounce largemouth bass back at Carrollton, Mississippi.
(And what can he do for an encore?)*

P.E.T.A. to the side though, most people I know say that "catch
and release" is really the only way to preserve fish for future
generations. To simply catch and kill everything you catch is not a
very good idea. Sure, you may have a big family or a bunch of
hungry neighbors, but all too often, an angler will return home with
dozens of fish and may wind up burying them in the backyard as
fertilizer. That is indeed a terrible thing to do. Some alleged
"sportsmen" will go out with bow and arrow, Robin Hood style, and
murder a mess of carp. Sure, if they eat them, I guess that's okay,
but many of these guys view what they are doing as sport and who
cares about the fish!

Catch and Release is the rule rather than the exception among
clubs like Trout Unlimited, BassMasters, The Carp Anglers Group,
and many more. I heartily agree and support such efforts and hope

you too will put many back alive.

Now, how to do that? Go back to Chapter NINE, Hook removal. Get the pair of scissors and the hemostat (straight metal frame, not bent). Some fishermen will bend the barbs down on their hooks and that makes removal very easy if the fish is lip hooked. The hemostat though will remove a barbed hook from a mouth with relative ease anyway. Yes, barbless hooks are a good idea, but the "two pair" is even better. Practice catch and release by removing the hook with hemostats if you can see the hook, or by cutting your line with the scissors if the hook is too far down in the fish's mouth or worse, throat or belly. Clearly, there are some fish that may die from the stress involving the fight and position of the hook, but the overwhelming majority of what you release as just described will live to eat another day.

"Catch and release" ... try it! Not only will you find it rewarding, your little companion may also think that you both are pretty nice people.

By the way, since so many fish are either undersized, over a bag limit, or out of season, you had better know how to put such critters back alive anyway, or else the guy with the shiny badge might have to write you up. You need to know which fish have to be released, for sure.

CHAPTER 18

Mounting

To mount or not to mount? That is the question. Some of you will want to throw everything back and others may insist on keeping every legal fish they catch to take home to eat. Then in the middle are those who want a "trophy" on their wall. On charter and head boats, your mate will always know a company nearby that will provide you with such service. Honestly, the mounting company may give a small percentage of their income back to the mate or skipper as a commission, but that is not important. After all, if you wanted such a thing, how else would you have found out about its availability?

There are two schools of thought. One involves what is called a "Skin Mount." The taxidermist takes your cold and well kept fish and generally freezes it, but before doing so, they will take full and complete measurements as well as a few full color photographs. When ready to do business, they will thaw it out, skin it, and prepare a mold to wrap the skin around.

Some do this with Plaster of Paris and others use very light-weight material such as Styrofoam. Whatever the material, they take very careful pains to have the skin tightly wrapped around the mold, and then begin the long process of painting. You see, much of the skin color will have disappeared, so the expert will have to revert back to photos to try and duplicate the color of the fish when it just came out of the water.

The other style involves creating a mounted fish completely out of the measurements taken by the mate on the boat with the fish usually being released. Color photos of the fish as it was just landed will help immeasurably. Length and girth are key. The taxidermist is an artist of sorts and can usually create a virtual exact duplicate of your fish this way. You have the choice of putting the wonderful fish back and still having a duplicate of it to hang on your study wall, or knowing that you have a true "skin mount," it's up to you. Either way, make sure you have an experienced hand taking care of this because your tuna could come back shaped like an eel!

CHAPTER 19

Find A Friend

L ifelong partners as well as old-fashioned buddies can be met on the water, and if you share the joys of fishing together, an excellent opportunity of meeting someone who you can bond with for life exists.

Frankly, when I am on the water, I am a fishing lunatic, and even if my buddy Ron Bern is in the boat, we don't talk much, because my concentration level is so extreme. You don't have to be a nut case like me, and can enjoy the sport at whatever level you chose to. If you want to view it as a social event, that's fine with me. When I am on a headboat filled with other fisherpersons, and the lines are over the rail, you may be able to count my spoken words on one hand. Other than a loud yell periodically (I hope) that goes something like this: "Get the gaff," or "Get the net," or maybe "You are fishing too doggone close to me" — or maybe an indecipherable grunt when I am really cranky. But you, on the other hand, may meet that special person on a fishing trip. It happens very, very often.

I fished with a charter boat captain in Texas who had been divorced twice. He had run a headboat out of California years before which stayed out at sea for weeks at a time. On board was a twice-divorced woman who was the ship's cook, and they have lived happily ever after! Over the years, I have run across dozens of hooked up couples who met while fishing.

If you aren't after a life partner, fishing still is a great way to meet friends. A fishing buddy can help share driving and other expenses, and in general, unless you are as far out there as I am, can really work out great.

CHAPTER **20**

Still More

Lateral Line Vs. "Vibration Time"

Since you are a "beginner," chances are 99-1 that you never heard of a "lateral line." Before I read up on this I wrote about something that I called "Vibration Time." And it turned out that I was writing about something that had its own name and simple explanation, doggone it!

As you fillet any fish, you will see that a line runs laterally across both of its sides, from head to tail. The meat of a fish is far heavier above this line than below. Just about every fish has a layer of blood right beneath its skin that is thickest at this line. Called "lateral line" for good reason, it runs laterally from one end to the other.

Scientists have explained that this line serves as a conductor of knowledge to fish. Call it an appetite "G-Spot" if you want, but when the lateral line of any fish is tweaked, it usually has an extreme attitude adjustment.

What normally tweaks the line is vibration. So when I started calling this "Vibration time," I was right, but it already had an explanation. Vibration of a fish nearby that is attacking a smaller prey will get any fish in the neighborhood interested. If a few baitfish see a bigger fish and change direction and speed up in an attempt to escape, a critter that may not even be hungry may all of a sudden decide it's time to eat.

More times than I can even dream to count, I have been some-where, on land, wading, or on a boat, and dead quiet conditions became a frenzy of activity. There may be a bunch of rods in use at different angles and depths when a rod that is rigged with a slider float at 12 feet down, cast 50-75 feet away from the boat, gets whacked. Next thing you know, the drag on rod two that is laying dead on bottom, right under the boat, a full 150-200 feet away, goes screaming off. Simply, the fish at bottom sensed the fact that the other fish was attacking food and it's little pea-brain appetite alarm was triggered into action.

Sure, fish travel in schools but I'm not talking about that. I'm talking about fish that are nowhere near each other deciding to eat at virtually the same moment. That is "Vibration Time," a/k/a lateral line time.

I talked to veteran skipper Bob Murphy in Texas about this while gathering pictures for the book. I fished with him in the winter and did very well. He targets my favorite fish, hybrid bass, in Lake Conroe and we talked about how a bunch of baits really trigger the fish into a frenzy.

I've experienced this often and one such location is called "The Race" in Long Island Sound. Here a group of anglers drop whole herring down into turbid water while attached to extra heavy sinker/harness rigs called "drails." While bluefish and striped bass (the fish most commonly caught this way) do travel in schools, they are often driven into a feeding frenzy because other members of their group eat up a storm. The group fishing creates what seems like a school of bait and the rest is history.

Well, Bob trolls a group of lines with live bait and in the late spring through the summer, he usually produces limit catches of five hybrids per angler within an hour of starting to fish. He feels that hybrid bass (among other fish) really go nuts when they see or sense another fish attacking bait. And when their neighbor eats, so too do they. This is a clear example of what I call "Vibration Time!" Bob will catch fish on occasion while pulling only one line but when he simulates a school of bait, the fish come gathering to the slaughter.

Solunar Time

As opposed to "Vibration Time," another often predictable time that fish will bite is called "Solunar Time." While a scientist can better explain what lateral lines are all about, they too can probably let you know the real meaning of "Solunar Time." It all has to do with the way that the sun and moon line up.

Sure, once you develop your angling skills, you may find out that fish feed much less during periods of extremely high barometer. And just before it starts to drop steeply, fish often go on an eating binge.

Full moon triggers certain fish into hungry beasts and other fish will go nearly off their feed at such times. In particular, if a clear sky is present during a full moon, fish can feed all night long. As with us humans, if they are stuffed, they are just that, full, and many fish will not eat during the day because of that.

None of the above examples have anything to do with "Solunar Time." This involves those times of day (it takes place four times) when fish feed more aggressively than other times. Add birds flying and animals on the prowl at much the same time and you are left with a fact that many of us believe most strongly in. Somehow or another, when the sun and moon are in just the right relationship to each other, the pressure in the atmosphere that this causes seems to turn fish, animals, and birds "on!"

During a 24-hour period, there are two times before and another two after noon when this occurs. Twice a day it will be for 90-120 minutes and the other two times it will take place for only a half-hour. These are called, respectively, "Peak Periods" (longer) and "Minor Periods" (shorter). I have personally experienced this countless times.

If a peak period is scheduled for 11 am, I will try to be all set up in place before 11. Other than during extreme and sudden weather changes, it is predictable that fish will suddenly start to feed with extreme aggression for that 1½ to 2 hour period! And you ask me "Why?" don't you. Well, honestly, I don't know why but I'm here to tell you that it really works. The better tackle stores and mail order houses have peak period charts that you can buy.

One is printed by a company with a name like "Knights." You may also be able to find a daily Solunar Table via your computer.

Checklist

A "checklist" is something I saved for the very last. Always have a camera with you in case you catch a fish that you want to release but still have something to remember it by. A photo is far better than trying to rely on memory alone. A scale could be helpful here as well as a tape measure, but even with them both, hey, what is better than a color picture? Tough to arrange for if you are alone, but carry one anyway.

Safety is extremely important, of course. Sure, beginners should know how to swim. They need to have at least a minor working knowledge of first aid as well as a first aid kit. Their boat should contain the required number of Coast Guard approved life jackets. A whistle or other sound-making device is urgently needed. What if your engine dies or you get stuck in a fog with no fuel left in the tank? A compass has to be way on top of your list but before you head out on the water, you will need to know how to read it as well as what compass reading is needed to get back to your launch site. Know where each closest point of land is, in case you cannot see and only your compass will help you reach shore.

Before you even launch the boat, make sure your electric motor's battery was newly charged and the gas engine can is full. A spare tire for your boat trailer, if applicable, is another on the "must have" list in case you get a flat.

And if you will use live bait, carry two bait nets because more often than you could imagine, you may drop one overboard. If you want to keep a few fish, by all means, carry a net with you. If the goal is sissy-sized stream trout, then have one of those over the shoulder ones. But if beasts are possible, be certain to have a net that you can fit "Jaws" into, please.

Now throw in a ruler, pair of scissors and a hemostat, plus seasick pills, and regardless of the weather forecast, a lightweight set of foul weather gear. And clearly, carry a tube of reel oil and maybe even some of that spray stuff like "WD40." It not only works to free up tight connections — some fishermen feel that if you spray it on your lure or bait, it even attracts some fish!

Hey look, while you may be a "beginner," the goal here is to give you enough detail to build up your confidence in yourself so as to allow you to enjoy our hobby.

"Beginner" or newly returned to this sport "casual angler," I hope you learned from this book. In particular, if you are just about ready to retire or have recently retired, use this book as something to let you know that something really wonderful lies ahead. Worrying about what to do with your time may be for some. For you though, fishing can and should be the answer. If you can walk, with or without a cane or crutches, or if someone can push your chair, go fishing. If you can or maybe cannot see, fishing still will be a wonderful means of getting fresh air and plenty of pleasure out of life.

I have fished with 90+ year old anglers who seem to drop years during the outing. Yes, they may not be able to reel in the monsters of the sea any longer, but just being on the water alone may be their salvation.

See you on the water, kiddo, be you 4 or 94!

Scuze me, gone fishin'.

Index

A

Abercrombie & Fitch 41

Adult Education classes 13

Aging With Style 127

American Sportfishing Association 9

anchor 33, 57-61, 63-64, 74, 88

anchoring 7, 32, 57, 59, 63, 65

anglers 9-10, 13, 15, 22, 32, 34, 38-39, 41, 45-46, 55, 57, 61, 66-68, 82, 84, 93, 95-96, 99, 112-113, 115, 122, 125

anise 25

anti-barf 19

B

backing 51

backlash 45, 53

bagel 27

bait 6-7, 15-17, 21, 24-29, 31, 35-36, 39, 41-42, 45-47, 52, 55, 57, 61-62, 67-69, 76, 82-83, 87-89, 93, 99-100, 108, 122, 124, 125

Bait & Tackle 16

bait-casting 35-36, 46

baked 111

balance 7, 46, 50-51, 53

bale 53

bamboo 35, 41

bank 8, 22, 66, 83, 95-96, 105

barb 70, 100

Barbara 19

barracuda 99

barrel 8, 62, 98-99, 101-102

BassMasters 115

beak 100

Berkley 26

Bern, Ron 119

Bernie's Fishing Tackle 4

birds nest 35

block tin squids 92

bluefish 89, 97, 99, 122

boats 7, 18, 45, 47, 60-62, 75, 78-86, 98, 117

bobbers 8, 82, 93

boots 72, 74-75

Boy Scout 100

brackish 56

braided 35, 45, 55

bridle 7, 60-61, 63, 65

broiled 111

Brooklyn 4, 15

bucket 29

butterfish 97

buzz baits 93

C

California 86, 119

Can Man 6, 34

Canada 9, 72

canoe 57, 78-79

Captain Morgan's B&T 4

carp 24-27, 33, 37, 46, 66, 115

Carp Anglers Group 115

Carpworld 127

cash 17

casting 7, 35-38, 40, 42-43, 45-47, 50, 52-53, 82, 89, 92

catch and release 8, 114-116

catfish 22, 25-28, 32, 66, 96

chain 16, 58-59

charter 7, 17-18, 21, 45-47, 80, 84, 89, 103, 117, 119

charters 13, 18

cheese 26

chocolate 25

chum pot 32

chumming 6, 8, 32-33, 89

circle hook 68, 70, 99

cleaning 8, 103, 105, 107

clinch (knot) 8, 62, 101

closed face 37

clothing 7, 72-73, 75-77, 95

clubs 13, 112, 115

Coast Guard 78, 84-85, 124

codfish 48, 105

cold 7, 15, 26, 67, 72-75, 77, 84, 107, 117

Coney Island 15

conventional 7, 35-39, 47, 52, 55, 106

cooking 8, 108-111

cooler 29, 107

corn 6, 10, 24, 27, 32

cornmeal 6, 25

coverall 75

crabs 88

crawfish 6, 29, 31

crayfish 31

Crossing their eyes 68

curly-queue 100

current 17, 61, 63-64, 66, 83, 87-89, 95, 97

D

Dacron 35, 55, 92

Danforth 58-59, 63

dead bait 6, 27

Del Rossi, Captain Pete 88

Denmark 48

Denny's Guide Service 4, 14, 86

Department of Fish and Game 16

diesel 81, 87

dipsey 96

double-anchoring 7, 57, 59, 63

doughballs 6, 24-25

downrigger 55, 62

downstream 38, 56, 63-64, 66, 83

drag 6, 25, 37, 39-40, 43-44, 48, 54, 62, 69, 83, 122

drails 122

drift 55, 61, 85-88, 90, 97

drift boats 85-86

drifting 7, 61, 87-88

dry fly 44

Dry Tortugas 22

E

East Coast Angler 127

eel 31, 118

eels 31

egg 8, 26, 62, 89, 95-96, 98, 111

egg sinkers 8, 96

egg skeins 26

electricity 48-49

engines 7, 81, 88

England 22

F

ferrules 35, 41

fiberglass 43, 47, 79

fillet 105-108, 110-111, 121

Fish 'N Tales 4, 94

fish finder 59, 65

Fishing & Hunting News 127

fishing derbies 7, 66

fishing derby 4, 67

fixed spool 6, 37-38, 53

flatfish 105, 110

fleunder 29

flies 7-8, 10, 44, 76-77, 93

floats 8, 17, 26-27, 44, 82, 93-95

Florida 4, 12, 22, 75, 85-86

flounder 99, 105

fluorocarbon 55, 98-99

fly 4, 6-7, 35, 37-45, 48, 50-53, 55, 66, 93, 101

fly rods 6-7, 41, 43

food 19, 22, 32, 66-67, 91-92, 105, 108, 122

forceps 41

Fortescue 88

foul weather gear 76, 124

Franklin, Benjamin 48

freebies 32-33

freshwater 6-7, 23-24, 26-27, 31-33, 45, 52, 54-57, 59, 61-63, 65, 67, 72, 74, 77-79, 81, 83, 91, 95, 98-99, 112

fried 8, 108

friend 8, 11, 16, 37, 41, 48, 60, 63, 79, 110, 112, 119-120

full moon 123

G

gall bladder 105

Galveston 66

George's Bank 22, 105

gloves 74

golf 22

Gone Fishin'...With Kids 16

government 16, 113

graphite 43-44, 48-49

Gray, Zane 93

Great Britain 9, 16, 66

Great Lakes 62, 80, 92

H

halibut 14, 28, 45

hand warmers 73

Hat Insurance 77

Hawaii 47

headboats 18, 21

heart 6, 17, 28, 31, 110-111

hemostats 41, 71, 116

herring 33, 57, 122

hip boots 75

hook 4, 7, 9, 17, 21-22, 24-25, 28, 31, 42, 51, 62, 66, 68-71, 76, 89-90, 92-94, 97-101, 116

hook removal 7, 22, 71, 116

Houston 66

hybrid bass 27, 57, 66, 97, 104, 109, 122

I

in-line 93

Internet 16

Italy 35

J
jerkbait 92
jig 61, 89, 93
Johnboat 57, 78-79
juniors 6, 15

K
K.I.S.S. 54
kids 1, 3, 6, 16, 19-21, 27, 29, 67, 96, 113
king mackerel 99
knots 8, 58, 100

L
Lake Conroe 4, 104, 109, 122
lakes 7, 16, 56, 62, 80-82, 93
land 8, 11, 13, 32, 37, 77, 82, 89, 95, 98, 107, 122, 124
largemouth bass 66, 115
lateral line 8, 105, 121-122
leaders 8, 41, 44, 55, 98-100
left hand 39
level-wind 6, 36, 51
library 13, 15, 45
license 8, 84, 112-113
life jacket 78
life partner 120
liver 6, 27
Long Island Sound 122
Louisiana 31
Luftglass Green Rock Flop 41
Luftglass, Manny 3-4, 41, 134
lure 28, 38-39, 42, 45, 53, 61, 66, 68-69, 76, 82-83, 92-93, 97, 99, 101, 125

M
macho kids 6, 21
Manny Madness 22
marbles 33
marshmallows 6, 26-27
Massachusetts 86, 89
mate 28, 55, 84, 87, 100, 103, 105, 107, 117-118
metal pole 58, 82
Mexico 22, 66
minnows 29
Moby Tree 61
monofilament 34, 44, 54
mounting 8, 117
Murphy, Bob 4, 104, 109, 122
Murphy's Guide Service 4
muskellunge 66
mutton snapper 97

N
Navy 74, 100
neoprene 75
net 63, 71, 94, 119, 124
New England 22
New Jersey 3-4, 31, 88, 115
New Mexico 66
New York 4, 41, 47, 66, 73, 85, 106
Nick Jr 127
night crawler 31
NJ Division of Fish & Wildlife 4
non-offset 99-100
noodle-rods 45
North American Fisherman 127
Norway 29

nylon 35, 58

nymph 44

O

O. Mustad & Son 4

obstructions 7, 65

offset 29, 99-100

oil 6, 41, 76, 108, 110-111, 124

open boat 103

open faced 37

Opening Day 22

Orvis 41

outrigger 62

oxygen 29

P

P.E.T.A. 114-115

pack rod 48

party boats 47

pawl and sprocket 43

pay ponds 7, 16-17, 66

pay waters 16

Penn 4, 37-38, 41, 50

Penn Fishing Tackle 4

Penn Reels 38

Pennsylvania 30, 66, 94

Perrone, Joe 4, 6, 16, 41-42

pier 15, 29, 33, 35, 77

Pig'n jig 93

pike 93, 99

pinch-on 8, 97

pink shrimp eggs 26

Planer Board 62

plastic 29, 37, 48, 82, 87, 91-93, 98, 107

plugs 91-92

pole 6, 35, 46, 58, 62, 69, 82

pond 16-17, 35, 56, 63, 66-67, 76, 96

pork rind 93

Power Bait 6, 26

protected water 18

pyramid 8, 89, 95

R

Ray's Guide Service 4

reel 6-7, 10, 17, 34-41, 43-46, 50-55, 62, 68-69, 83, 89, 92, 97-99, 124-125

Reference Librarian 13, 15

reservoir 57

retired 6, 11-12, 125

revolving spool 6, 35

Rhode Island 86

River Anchor 63

rivers 7, 28, 56, 63, 78

rod 7, 10, 17, 19, 33-34, 38-39, 41, 43-51, 53, 55, 60-62, 68-70, 82, 87, 90, 94-95, 99, 122

rods 6-7, 15, 35, 41, 43, 45-48, 57, 61, 69, 82, 112, 122

rotate fish 8, 89

rubber-core 97

Rutgers University Press 127

S

safe water 78

safety 80, 124

sailfish 53, 93

salmon 6, 26-28, 45, 62, 64, 70, 73, 86, 92, 108

saltwater 7-8, 10, 27-28, 31, 36, 44, 47, 54, 56, 61, 73, 77, 80-81, 84-85, 87, 89, 91-93, 95, 97, 99, 101, 112-113

San Diego 22

Sandy Hook Bay 31

sautéed 8, 110-111

scaler 107

Schmitz, Mike 4, 64

Schoerlin, Captain Judie 4

scissors 71, 116, 124

sea gulls 57

sea trout 88

seasick 18-19, 124

senior citizens 13, 113

shedder crab 28

SHH 17, 19, 27-29, 41, 48, 58, 64, 73, 77, 80, 82-83, 87-88, 90, 105, 110

shiners 33

shrimp 6, 26, 28-29, 31, 88, 100

silver hake 15

simmered 110

single-anchoring 7

sinkers 8, 41, 47, 67, 89, 95-97

skin mount 117-118

Skylands Visitor 127

slack 63, 68-69

sleep 19

slider float 94-95, 122

slingshot 33

slip-bobber 95

slope 7, 59, 65, 81

smallmouth bass 27

snelled 97, 100

soft lures 8, 92

solunar time 8, 123

sonar 81, 87

spin-cast 7, 37-38, 46, 53

spinner 93

spinners 93

spinning reels 37-39, 45, 53-54

spool 6, 35-38, 40, 42, 51-54, 59, 89

sportsmen 115

Sportsmen's Series 127

squeamish kids 6, 20-21

Steeplechase Pier 15

stickbait 91-92

streamer 44

streams 7, 41, 63, 78

striped bass 27, 31, 47, 98, 122

sturdy 80

Styrofoam 29, 79, 117

sunfish 21, 27, 99

surf 46-47, 89, 95

sushi 108

sweetwater 28, 32, 54, 93, 96-97, 100

swivel 62, 93, 97-99, 101

T

tackle 4, 6-8, 16, 22, 34-35, 37, 39-41, 43-45, 47, 49-50, 52, 73, 82, 91, 93, 95, 97, 99-101, 113, 123

taper 42-43, 45-46

taxidermist 117-118

tennis 22, 93

terminal tackle 7-8, 44, 82, 91, 93, 95, 97, 99, 101

Texas 66, 72, 104, 109, 119, 122

The Anglers News 127

The Fisherman Magazine 127

The Fisherman's Trader 127

The Race 122

thermal 72, 74-75

thermal underwear 72

three-way swivels 8, 97

tilefish 55

tip 42-43, 45, 50, 68-69, 80, 87, 105

tippet 41, 44

tipsy 78

Titanic 19

toilet 21

trolling 7, 54, 61, 63, 69-70, 81

trophy 117

trout 17, 24, 26-27, 30, 41-45, 48, 53, 62, 66, 69-70, 82, 88, 93, 97, 106, 115, 124

Trout Unlimited 45, 115

tuna 50, 52, 89, 108, 118

two-pair 71

U

U.S. Fish and Wildlife Service 9

ultra-lite 46

Uncle Josh 26

underwear 72

United Kingdom 46, 108

United States 4, 10, 28, 33, 37

V

vanilla 24-26

vibration 8, 60, 121-123

volunteer 11-12

W

waders 41, 75

watch cap 74

waterproof 72, 74-75

weakfish 88-89

weedless 92-93

white 6, 25, 27-29, 35, 54, 76, 93, 95, 105-106, 109

whiting 15

wind 6, 18-19, 33, 36, 51, 59-61, 63, 77, 80, 87-88, 97, 107, 115

winter 15, 66, 72-73, 77, 122

wire 54-55, 98-99

wool 75

worm 24, 30

worms 6, 31, 100

About The Author

Manny Luftglass has written his column, "Gone Fishin'" for a wide variety of newspapers since 1971. This is his 12th book. Two were published by Rutgers University Press and he self-published all ten others, including this one.

His credentials include being published in dozens of newspapers, plus feature articles in *The Anglers News, East Coast Angler, The Fisherman Magazine, The Fisherman's Trader, Skylands Visitor, Carpworld* (England), and its equivalent in Germany, *North American Fisherman, Sportsmen's Series, Fishing & Hunting News, Nick Jr.,* and *Aging With Style.*

Order Form

For additional copies of this book, any of the ten other *Gone Fishin'* books, or my book, *So You Want To Write A Book*, please send check or money order to:

Gone Fishin' Enterprises
PO Box 556
Annandale, NJ 08801

- New Jersey residents please add 6% state sales tax.
- Tell me who you'd like the book autographed to.
- There will no shipping or handling charges.

For bulk orders call: 908 996-2145

Look up *Gone Fishin'* books at:
www.gonefishinbooks.com

Name: _____

Address: _____

City: _____ State: _____ Zip: _____

Autograph To: _____

Please send me:

# of Copies	Book Title	Price
_____	Gone Fishin'... With Kids ....$ 9.99	
_____	Gone Fishin'... In Spruce Run Reservoir $12.95	
_____	Gone Fishin'... For Carp $12.95	
_____	**Gone Fishin'... For Beginners $13.95**	
_____	So You Want To Write A Book $13.95	
_____	Gone Fishin'... In Round Valley Reservoir $13.95	
_____	Gone Fishin'... In Lake Hopatcong.....................$13.95	
_____	Gone Fishin'... The 50 Best Waters In Pennsylvania.....$13.95	
_____	Gone Fishin'... The 75 Best Waters In Connecticut $13.95	
_____	Gone Fishin'... In N.J. Saltwater Rivers And Bays $14.95	
_____	Gone Fishin'... The 100 Best Spots In New Jersey $16.00	
_____	Gone Fishin'... The 100 Best Spots In New York $16.00	